SOMETHING SACRED

In 1971 Mary Barnes published *Mary Barnes: Two Accounts of a Journey Through Madness.* The book had an enormous impact, and ran into numerous editions. It is probably the most celebrated contemporary account of what it is like to be mad. In it she described the experience of profound regression in London's best-known community household of the 1960s, Kingsley Hall. Her psychotherapist and co-author, Joseph Berke, described the experience in his own way. Mary Barnes slowly 'came up', and began to paint and write.

Something Sacred, through a series of interviews, continues the story, nearly twenty years later, and reproduces some of Mary Barnes' work. It describes her subsequent life and her involvement in a series of psychotherapeutic households, this time as a helper to others. In this book she looks back on the Kingsley Hall years with detachment, humour and gratitude. Her observations on problems of mental health care, on the relationship between psychotherapy and religious practice, and on the nature of deep regression will stimulate much thought.

Mary Barnes is a writer and painter. **Ann Scott** is the co-author (with Ruth First) of *Olive Schreiner* (The Women's Press, re-issued 1989). Formerly an editor at Free Association Books, she is now researching the work of women psychoanalysts.

D1514357

Mary Barnes, 1989

SOMETHING SACRED

Conversations, Writings, Paintings

Mary Barnes with Ann Scott

*'an association in which the free development of each
is the condition of the free development of all'*

Free Association Books / London / 1989

First published in Great Britain in 1989 by
Free Association Books
26 Freegrove Road
London N7 9RQ

British Library Cataloguing in Publication Data

Barnes, Mary, *1923–*
   Something sacred: conversations, writings,
   paintings.
   1. Schizophrenics – Biographies
   I. Title   II. Scott, Ann
   362.2
ISBN 1–85343–101–X

Typeset by BP Datagraphics, Bath

Printed and bound in Great Britain by
Short Run Press Ltd, Exeter

'For JOE'
Dr Joseph H. Berke

Mary Barnes

CONTENTS

CONTENTS

LIST OF ILLUSTRATIONS

Black and white section

1 Mary Barnes and Joe Berke, the attic, Hampstead, 1971
2 Painting *Peter the Fisherman* at Kingsley Hall, 1968
3 *Three Stages of Sacrifice: The Lamb in Fire, Christ on the Cross, Christ as the Host (Consecrated)*, 1969. This painting was originally on the dining-room wall at Kingsley Hall.
4 *Crucifixion*, wall of my room on the roof, Kingsley Hall, January 1966
5 *Foetal-like Figures*, wall of my room on the roof, Kingsley Hall, January 1966
6 *The Cross of Christ*, Kingsley Hall, December 1969
7 *Nativity*, Saint Dympna's, Seaton, Devon, 1980

Colour section

1 *Tree*, the door of my room, Kingsley Hall, 1968
2 Chagford, front door, 1976
3 Scroll of the *Hollow Tree*, St Andrews, 1987
4 *Disintegration*, Kingsley Hall, April 1966
5 *The Temptation of Christ*, Kingsley Hall, April 1966
6 *Resurrection*, Kingsley Hall, July 1967
7 *The Ascension*, Kingsley Hall, September 1967

INTRODUCTION
Ann Scott

TO PUBLISH A BOOK of conversations with Mary Barnes nearly twenty years after her account of breakdown and 'coming up' is to pose a number of questions about mental health, psycho-therapy and writing about experience. Even more acutely, the question of 'readership' is posed. For just as Mary Barnes' own life until Kingsley Hall involved an unhappy career in nursing, psychiatric hospitalization and chronic alienation, so one cannot separate that experience from the fascination which her account of that experience exerted on a generation of readers. *Mary Barnes: Two Accounts of a Journey Through Madness*, jointly authored by Mary and her therapist Joseph Berke, was first pub-lished in 1971 and subsequently translated into seventeen lan-guages. It formed the basis of David Edgar's play *Mary Barnes*, first performed in London in 1979 and since then staged around the world. It forms the starting point for *Something Sacred*, which aims to be both a sequel in time and a reflection back on an earlier narrative. In this introduction, then, I want to consider the impact of that earlier narrative, and to put into context some of the issues raised in *Something Sacred*.

For readers who are meeting Mary Barnes for the first time, some words of background. Joseph Berke is an American physician and psychotherapist who first came to London in the early 1960s to study with the psychiatrist and psychoanalyst R. D. Laing, then achieving celebrity and influence as the author of *The Divided*

Self (Laing, 1960), a theoretical critique of existing conceptualiza-
tions of psychosis, especially schizophrenia. The book argued
for the meaningfulness or psychic lawfulness of psychotic states,
concerning itself with the social – that is, the family – context
of schizophrenia.* By this time Berke had completed his medical
training in New York but had no wish to pursue a career in
conventional psychiatry. Laing was extending his theoretical
critique and was actively trying to set up a community in which
the usual doctor–patient distinctions would not apply, and where
a few people who elected to do so could undergo, with assistance
and 'life support', a process of profound disintegration and spontaneous reintegration of their personality.

Based on the view that psychosis was potentially a healing
experience (Barnes and Berke, 1971, p. 94), such a household
would provide an alternative to the custodial and pharmacological
approach of the conventional mental hospital, and Berke was
invited to participate in the experiment. Long before meeting
Mary Barnes, Joe Berke writes, he had begun to realize that
mental illness was not an illness or sickness, but reflected what
was happening in a disturbed and disturbing group of people.
Such a view rejected wholesale the medical model in psychiatry,
and was in harmony with Laing's thought. Thus in *Mary Barnes*
Berke's key formulation is the following: 'Experiences occurring
in persons labelled schizophrenic and commonly subsumed under
the term "psychosis" are not at all unintelligible, that is, crazy.
They simply occur at a different order of reality, akin to a waking

---

* In this introduction I am using the words 'psychosis' and 'psychotic'
in the conventional descriptive sense that covers gross disturbance in
the content and form of thought, perception, affect, sense of self, volition
and relationship to the external world (APA, 1980, p. 182). Part of
this, incidentally, coincides with Mary Barnes' own current definition:
'My understanding of "psychotic" is that it is an experience of a divorce
from external reality' (see below, p. 90), and with the lay usage of
'crazy' or 'mad'. A consideration of the wider question of treating
mental disorders as primarily disturbances in an interpersonal field is
beyond the scope of my introduction.

dream' (Barnes and Berke, 1971, p. 84). And just as a dream carries a latent as well as manifest content, one might add, so schizophrenia bears its own coded meaning.

Mary Barnes, an English nurse then in her early forties, and with a long history as a diagnosed schizophrenic, was 'holding on' for the household, so that she could 'get back inside my Mother, to be reborn, to come up again, straight, and clear of the mess' (Barnes and Berke, 1971, p. 13). Paralleling the intensity of this stated need, R. D. Laing's directive to her before the place was found is memorable: 'You need analysis twenty-four hours out of twenty-four. You will be like a child and cannot be around like that. You would only get locked up – in a mental hospital. What there is of you is very frail. You can't lie on a couch to have analysis and get up and carry on' (Barnes and Berke, 1971, p. 69). Memorable at two levels: it speaks to the limitations both of mental hospital and of analysis when someone is truly 'mad' (Laing himself speaks of her mad state). Secondly, it posits the need, in certain forms of madness, for a special kind of place in which to live. In the context of the later work of the Philadelphia Association (an organization which grew out of the work of Laing and his collaborators), it anticipates the establishment of therapeutic households: places which might restore the 'proper' function of the mental hospital as an asylum from the pressures of the external world (Barnes and Berke, 1971, p. 94). *Something Sacred* shows how this work has been continued, both by the Philadelphia Association (PA) and by the Arbours Association (established by Joseph Berke and Morton Schatzman in 1970), and now by Mary Barnes in her work with the Shealin Trust in Scotland (see below, pp. 33–8).

As its subtitle implies – *Two Accounts of a Journey Through Madness* – *Mary Barnes* was not one but two versions of one person's regressive breakdown and gradual reintegration of self; the book constructs (and reconstructs) dual perceptions of the 'same' experiences. It is in the very gap between these sets of perceptions that much of the interest of the book lies: both authors acknowledge that they are relying on memory, and there are inevitable discrepancies. There is no single authorial voice, and so there is no closure. Mary Barnes' sections grip the reader's attention by their capacity to evoke minute variations in mood or impulse, and by the very primitiveness of their emotional field. Joseph Berke's sections have a broader point of reference as they include a fast-moving discussion of training in psychiatry, the 'proper' role of the psychiatrist, and the nature of the therapist's relationship with the person he or she is assisting. 'One cannot assume knowledge of another's interpersonal field, nor prejudge peculiar behaviour as ''sick'' ' (Barnes and Berke, 1971, p. 86). The justification for this refusal of categories would, then, be the story recounted in *Mary Barnes*: of Mary's slow, spontaneous turn towards creativity after long periods of lying in bed, taking almost no nourishment, and using her shit to smear the walls of Kingsley Hall in breast-like shapes. Her newfound writing and painting was usually religious in imagery. 'Watching her [paint] was a great thrill', Berke writes, of the period when her themes included saints, devils, biblical stories and landscapes.

> Never once did she stop or look up although, as she worked, she would often laugh, or talk with or even scream at this or that figure ... as the figure began to make his presence known in the painting. From time to time a beautiful smile would break across her face. It was as if, at that moment, she had transcended all her troubles and entered an ecstatic reverie. (Barnes and Berke, 1971, p. 264)

Mary Barnes thus conveyed the most powerful of messages: that ordinary modes of coping in conventional society, and ordinary modes of practising and consuming institutional psychiatry were intensely destructive, if not psychically lethal. One finds this sense of 'near-death' in Mary Barnes' account of her years before Kingsley Hall, not only as an account of a life unlived, and of her active suicidality, but in her despondent acquiescence in her situation. 'It was a chronic ward', she writes of her mental hospital experience. 'It seemed they couldn't cure me. Always to be there, mad. In a despairing way I accepted it, wanting only to lie still in the dark, in the pads' (Barnes and Berke, 1971, p. 54). One finds this message, too, in Berke's account of misperception and misconstrual on a psychiatric admissions unit.

It concentrates on the steps by which a person's career as a patient is inaugurated, as in the scenario of a young girl admitted because of bizarre behaviour. When the situation is looked at interpersonally, it becomes clearer that it is the mother's hysteria about the odd, but arguably harmless, behaviour which leads the professional staff to confine the young girl. The parallel between family dynamics and psychiatry, then, is a form of invidious scapegoating: as in families so in psychiatry the individuals designated as patients carry the disturbance of the family group. 'We all knew', Berke comments acidly, 'that the mental hospital was simply an institutionalized extension of the family living-room, or maybe bedroom' (Barnes and Berke, 1971, p. 93). It is in the context of this critique of existing provision for the relief of mental distress that *Mary Barnes* unfolds.

Kingsley Hall was designed to be the alternative to the mental hospital that I have mentioned. It was a large settlement house in the East End of London in which Mary Barnes lived between 1965 and 1970. For different periods of time Joe Berke lived there, as did Laing, other members of the Philadelphia Association including the American physicians Leon Redler and Morton Schatzman (see Cooper *et al.*, 1989; Schatzman, 1972) and a number of other residents. Kingsley Hall was both a community, and a symbol for the wider countercultural movement of the 1960s that brought together groups of radicals in a range of interventions at the political, social, cultural and therapeutic levels. (Berke describes this phenomenon in a vivid and humorous account of a typical day at Kingsley Hall [Barnes and Berke, pp. 277–83].) The language of radicalism of the time proclaimed connections between social violence and the intimate violence of family life, and Mary Barnes' portrait of her family of origin – a suburban family in which her mother did not work outside the home and her father worked as a laboratory electrician – appealed to this political consciousness. Although Mary herself was not a political

radical, what she summoned up was the concealed violence perpe-
trated by human beings on other human beings that was so much
a theme of Laing's early writings. This description of a family
background establishes one of the main themes of the book: the
gap between surface and depth in family life which is pathological,
which drives mad. Take, for example, Mary's opening lines:

> My family was abnormally nice. Friends, relations and neigh-
> bours thought that we all lived happily together . . . Mum and
> Dad were always considerate and polite to each other . . . They
> never shouted. The air was cold yet a storm was always brewing
> . . . Life was like ice, brittle ice. The whole family wanted
> this ice to melt, wanted to be loved. But we feared if the ice
> broke we would all be drowned. Violence and anger lurked
> beneath the pleasantries. (Barnes and Berke, 1971, p. 14)

It is this gap between surface and depth which structures Mary's
account of family dynamics. No account of a personal past is
innocent – it always bears its own interpretation – and Mary's
account is no different: it was written at the end of her years
in Kingsley Hall, after a long and intense relationship with both
Laing and Berke. So it resonates with the language of double-
binds – the contradictory signals and messages, given at different
levels, which lead to total confusion about how to act in any
given situation – and the awareness that 'mercifully I broke down,
went mad. There was no question of my hiding under a habit
[a reference to her earlier wish to become a nun], a false divided
self' (Barnes and Berke, 1971, p. 51).

Mary describes a childhood filled with guilt about not being
able to be a 'good child'; with unexpressed or unacknowledged
anger at her mother's inability to love her ('I violently loved
my mother and wanted her to cuddle me'); and a profound sense
of alienation from herself ('buried in a great big hard shell')
(Barnes and Berke, 1971, pp. 16, 26). It is an account of primitive
anxieties and aggressions that focus on her mother's confusions
over loving and hating babies; Mary's confusion about sex; her
fascination with and fear of her shit; her jealousy of her three

siblings. In the family system, however, not only does her mother stress all the time that 'we were a very *ordinary* family', but all is *covered over*. As the blurb of the Penguin edition put it: her childhood was spent in a 'quiet, respectable and totally destructive family'. It can be no accident that these opposites – 'covered' and 'raw' – appear so frequently in Mary's descriptive vocabulary. They are to be found in *Something Sacred* as well.

A second theme is the fear of truth – of a truth about the family. Her brother's breakdown at the age of sixteen spoke a truth about the family: 'He incarnated all the anger I felt but couldn't feel' (Barnes and Berke, 1971, p. 40). And given the frequently expressed view that Laing identified madness as a higher state, let me add that I think truth, here, denotes the 'truth of' a situation, not a 'superior reality'. I believe that what Mary is referring to is the process by which the denial of the 'deeper' subjective reality eventually breaks down. As this happens, so individual madness may emerge. Madness is not itself the higher state, is not sanity, but a necessary state if any genuine growth is to come, or the past be left behind. And this question of truth links with a third theme, which concerns the aetiology, relief and transformation of mental distress. It has already been hinted at in Laing's and Berke's remarks about mental hospital.

Much of the force of *Mary Barnes* derives from its unstinting, if with hindsight simplistic, critique of institutional psychiatry. The issue, as it presented itself to Laing and his research colleagues, was how much hospital damaged a person who entered psychosis. Or, put another way, how much it denied subjective truth. So let us look at Mary's experience as a voluntary patient in a West London mental hospital in 1952 (I shall describe the events leading to this hospitalization in the next section). In her own words:

They gave me insulin and pushed me about to keep me moving. Then I got electric shocks and was put in a padded cell . . . It was terrible to be touched. Noise disturbed me. Light was blinding. The pads on the chronic ward, where they moved

me to, had black walls. The only relief was to be alone in
the dark, curled up, like a baby in the womb. In those days
I knew of no such connection. (Barnes and Berke, 1971, p.
53)

This is an account of a person's alienation from what she later
perceives to have been her own drives, and of a mental hospital's
apparent inability to attend to her experience, rather to concentrate
on her behaviour: 'to keep me moving'.* To me, then, one of
the most moving moments in the book – indeed one of the book's
turning points – is Mary's description of her meeting with Dr
Theodor Werner, an analyst who was visiting the hospital.

He said my name, Mary. Something moved inside me. He
didn't have a white coat on ... *Without words*, he touched
something inside me. (Barnes and Berke, 1971, p. 54)

She continues:

That tiny bit of me that was not punishing me to death, but
that wanted to live, Dr Werner had got hold of ... We didn't
have discussions. *I hadn't got words.* He used very few.
(Barnes and Berke, 1971, p. 54, my emphases)

'He strengthened that tiny part so much that I got out of the
hospital'. A chance encounter which gave her the will to live,
and which Mary remembers in *Something Sacred* (p. 43), when
speaking of the launch of *Mary Barnes*. What I find significant
is the very simplicity of the experience. Is it an idealization of
a gifted analyst? I cannot know. What it calls to mind, rather,
is the capacity for relatedness, however tenuous, on the part of
very disturbed patients which the analyst Frieda Fromm-
Reichmann posited (see Gralnick, 1969, pp. 33–4); and which

---

* 'In the dimension of "behaviour", Laing [in *The Politics of Experience* (1967)] correctly notes that psychiatrists tend to pay attention
to behaviour to the exclusion of experience' (Siegler *et al.*, 1972, p.
105).

Laing also assumed (see Lidz, 1972, p. 124; Coles *et al.*, 1972, p. 167). A wordless encounter 'met' Mary's need to be reached. It enabled her to hold on for Kingsley Hall.

In order for the experiences or memories alluded to in *Something Sacred* to be self-explanatory, let me run briefly through the narrative content of *Mary Barnes*. Such an account necessarily leaves out much, most particularly Joe Berke's theorization of Mary's regression as a defensive manoeuvre; nor can it capture Mary's terse, compact writing style: plain syntax, short paragraphs, high-intensity emotion. I want to concentrate on the main chronological sequence.* So let me track back to the breakdown of Peter Barnes, Mary's brother.

As a young adult, Peter is certified insane; Mary is now a nurse, and she becomes a Catholic at the age of twenty-six. Oppressed by her impulses to hit her mother, however, she deteriorates, becoming 'unable to express any feeling in words . . . my speech seemed to have gone' (Barnes and Berke, 1971, pp. 51–2). She feels cut off and alone. She has electroconvulsive therapy (ECT) at the age of twenty-nine in 1952; gets out of the mental hospital as a result of Dr Werner's help, gets back into nursing, and begins to feel she needs psychoanalysis. Through the analyst James Robertson, whom she knows through her work as a nursing tutor, she meets R. D. Laing, waits for Kingsley Hall, and in this long period of intermittent employment finds great support in her relationship with Mother Michael, a nun who 'knew about the madness of schizophrenics' (Barnes and Berke, 1971, p. 71). As she puts it, 'the *force* of my being was demanding release into its truer, mad state'; a contrast, perhaps, with her retrospective sense of being alienated, in mental hospital, from her desire. Now she is suicidal, and living only on milk, spending long periods in bed playing with her shit,

---

* *Mary Barnes* is being republished by Free Association Books with new Introductions by its authors.

which brings relief. At her moment of greatest despair, the PA grouping finds Kingsley Hall, and she moves there in 1965, 'to have a breakdown'.

Mary's long central section, 'The Down Years', describes the early period there: her impulses to hit those significant to her, her fear of seeing her parents, her periods in bed – long stretches of time without leaving her room – her being fed as a baby. She is allowed to do whatever she wishes, with the exception of her request that she be tube-fed. She cannot, at this stage, differentiate herself from her therapist Joe Berke, and whenever he goes out she feels a bomb has fallen. Her language is again one of violent bodily aggression: 'Leon [Redler of the PA] was talking to Joe. Something is wrong, why am I all terrible . . . I'm all splintered, showering away' (Barnes and Berke, 1971, p. 134). She is slowly discovering (uncovering, perhaps) her jealousies.

Joe Berke introduces her to drawing and she first uses grease crayons and scrap paper; then she starts to paint. 'Painting got me together, my body and soul. All my insides came out through my hands and my eyes and all the colour' (Barnes and Berke, 1971, p. 145). She goes to a local sculpture class, and her work is shown to artists who are friends of Joe Berke's. And interestingly, at the very moment when her creativity is beginning to find expression she is also waging a war with her anger. Slowly she starts to feel that with Joe's help, 'the clutch of the past [is] coming out of me' (Barnes and Berke, 1971, p. 168); the resolution of her anger is beginning.

What was the origin of this anger? Much of it centres on her relationship with her mother and to feeding. 'The trouble with me had been my real Mother *hadn't* really wanted me to have it, food. She couldn't, she hated me. Yet told me she loved me, and wanted me to eat' (Barnes and Berke, 1971, p. 188). In taking food from Joe Berke and from Noel Cobb and Paul Zeal, also of the PA, 'the past was broken. They were not my Mother. New ideas set in . . . I could eat according to the needs of my own body.' Equally slowly, as she experiences herself as an individual separate from her mother (and from Joe), she becomes able to express choices about the most basic of things: an item of food, the colour of a piece of clothing; she begins to cook. This is the process of what she calls 'getting whole'. In all there are four periods of going down, as a result of which she is able to write: 'Since the spring of '67 I have grown up. To an increasing extent I have become much more involved with people both at Kingsley Hall and in the outside world. Also I have had two successful exhibitions of my paintings' (Barnes and Berke, 1971, p. 227).

'With Mary at Kingsley Hall', by Joe Berke, sets the stage for an understanding of how this process was accomplished. Berke's initial priority is to help Mary become aware of her anger. 'Mary continually attributed *to* me anger which was clearly hers' (Barnes and Berke, 1971, p. 242). He is on hand to offer comments and interpretations about her confusion of herself and others, and to help her work through her conflicting identifications. They are living in the same place, and the 'happenings of the day' give innumerable opportunities for her anger or jealousy to be aroused. Each incident could be relived or worked over. On one occasion, for example, Mary is shattered when Joe goes out to participate in a poetry reading in protest against the war in Vietnam. Berke's response shows how he worked as a therapist:

> In the morning we played 'peek-a-boo' and 'hungry bear' and 'dangerous shark'. Mary squeezed me as hard as she could (which was quite hard, I assure you), and I, in turn, squeezed her. This put her shattered body all back together again, and, from her point of view, mine as well. Similar incidents occurred over and over while Mary gradually learned that, when I went out, I did not leave her forever, and that, before I came back, her rage had not blown me apart. (Barnes and Berke, 1971, pp. 246–7)

In a nutshell, this was the nature of the interaction: a combination of talk and action, with suggestions that Mary leapt on. (His initial suggestion that she draw was based on a memory of an influential teacher of psychiatry he had known in New York who used painting to communicate with catatonic individuals.) As Mary becomes less regressed (in Berke's words, 'After Mary had finally decided to "come up"' [Barnes and Berke, 1971, p. 365]), and Berke has ceased to live at Kingsley Hall, Mary's and his relationship changes. She goes to his office for therapy, and by the summer of 1968, when Mary is up and about in the house, she begins to be a helper to a mad girl at Kingsley Hall, and then to another resident who has delusions. She travels to Paris for a weekend. In April 1969 her first exhibition takes place. Her brother comes to live at Kingsley Hall. 'In the future and with Joe's help', she writes, 'I myself look forward to helping people who are very regressed to go through the experience and come up again; as well as to paint and to write' (Barnes and Berke, 1971, p. 359). The book ends with Joe Berke's celebration of the opening of Mary's exhibit at Camden Arts Centre in London: 'Mary was completely at ease. She moved from this person to that, greeting and being greeted, with charm and dignity. It was an amazing performance for someone who but a couple of years before refused to leave her room during the day for fear of bumping into someone in the hallway' (Barnes and Berke, 1971, p. 369).

Something Sacred could not have had a simpler origin. In March 1988 an unostentatious card arrived from Mary Barnes: writing at Joe Berke's suggestion, she wondered if Free Association Books (FAB) would like to see her recent work. We met, and she expressed interest in doing a second book, a kind of 'Kingsley Hall twenty years on'. She showed me stories and small paintings and drawings; she had a listing of all the talks she had given over the years, the pieces she had written for magazines – medical student publications, local mental health newsletters – the media attention she had received, TV and radio programmes in which she had participated. She had scrapbooks of book and play reviews. She was involved with a mental health trust in Scotland.

When she asked for help with an autobiography I suggested that we make a series of tapes. The work of Laing, Kingsley Hall, *Mary Barnes* the book and the play – all this was part of the culture of the sixties and seventies. The programme of the original Royal Court Theatre production of the play, for example, includes an extract from one of Sheila Rowbotham's first and most luminous writings on authenticity and women's liberation, juxtaposed with quotations from Sartre on freedom, Joe Berke on the labelling of schizophrenics, and Raoul Vaneigem on class struggle and everyday life. How does Mary herself see the time? How does she think about Kingsley Hall now? About regression? It is part of FAB's project to say that critical practices like psychotherapy have a history, and to explore that history. Mary Barnes is part of such a history, and a second book would create for both Mary and her readers a space in which to think over these issues, and to see some of her writing and painting. From the beginning, then, I sensed that issues of recognition with hindsight, of thought and interpretation changing with the passage of time, would play a large part in our conversations. So they did.

Here are five conversations, taped in London between May and November 1988. They were fairly heavily edited by me, after discussions between Mary and me sitting over raw transcripts; a few sequences have been rearranged to establish a continuity of themes. Most repetition has been eliminated, although a small amount is inevitable. In some cases I have revised the formulation of my comments or questions if the spoken version appeared ambiguous or incomplete; Mary has extended a few of her responses. At the same time, I wanted to retain a sense of freshness, the freshness of talk, and especially a sense of the idiosyncrasies of Mary's speech. The aim has been to give this prose the feel of an encounter, an encounter between two people, two voices. We move from reflections on the original book to the directly autobiographical, then to wider issues of regression and therapeutic households, of how to talk to groups about breakdown, and lastly to the relationship between psychotherapy and religious practice, a discussion which deepens Mary's observations about faith and madness in the first book.

In editing and copy-editing we altered sentence structure only to lighten any awkwardness of rapid speech. As it happens, my model for this project as a whole was the format of the American rock newspaper, *Rolling Stone*, which includes tone of voice, gestures and incidental detail as an integral part of any published interview. Such features appear in this text in square brackets, and are my insertions, as are most of the footnotes and editorial interventions. The final text has been approved by both of us, as was this introduction. All names of individuals, other than those in the public domain like Laing, other members of the helping professions and published writers, have been changed to preserve confidentiality.

Mary Barnes has the compelling quality of a deep, lived-in experience, recounted, from their different perspectives, by its two protagonists. I knew that a second book would need to be different in kind. Mary Barnes was older, for a start; and she and I met initially as strangers. From the beginning I envisaged my role as that of an informed facilitator. Our tapes, accordingly, fell somewhere between interview and conversation; as we got to know one another, the conversational aspect got stronger and is, I think, reflected in the tempo of the five chapters that make up Part 1 of the book: an evolution from the shy, somewhat formal beginning in 'Reflections', to the concluding give-and-take of ' "Something Sacred" '. At the same time, thoughts about Guattari's critique of Kingsley Hall (Guattari, 1984), or Sedgwick's critique of Laing (Sedgwick, 1972), or Lemoine-Luccioni's use of Mary's impulse to hit her mother in *The Dividing of Women or Woman's Lot* (Lemoine-Luccioni, 1987) were not in my mind: intentionally so, for Mary was not on trial in our discussions. Mary herself feels that her form of celebrity was rather strange (see below, pp. 5–9) and our meetings focused on how she negotiated it. We did not consider the scholarly and critical literature that surrounds her and Kingsley Hall; her views on art criticism in *Something Sacred* will show the reader why.

The title of this book is drawn from the last line of *Mary Barnes*, in which Mary is describing the kind of community she would like to see set up after Kingsley Hall, a place which could offer its residents both psychotherapy and, if religious, the practice of their faith. 'That's the sort of place I want, something sacred, full of *love*' (Barnes and Berke, 1971, p. 378). In *Something Sacred* the reader finds out what has happened since Kingsley Hall closed its doors in 1970, the circuitous path which brought Mary to Scotland. We learn how the first book came to be written, and how she finally learned to 'accept the gap' between her parents and herself. We meet a temperate commentary on her place in Kingsley Hall from a woman who now recognizes that it is 'practically impossible', in states of extreme regression, to understand the anxiety one is provoking in fellow residents of a community household (see below, pp. 17–18) – a far cry from the furious 'baby' who thought people should go her way and could not bear difference. She smiles when she thinks back to her Kingsley Hall belief that everyone should go to 'Ronnie or Joe, as if there wasn't another therapist in the world' (see below, p. 38); as she acknowledges, she has gained considerable detachment from the period.

We, also, are returning to the Kingsley Hall period after some twenty years and more. Much has happened in the mental health field in that time: there has been deinstitutionalization in psychiatry and the move to community care; the vicissitudes of the therapeutic community movement (see Oakley, C., 1989); the availability of effective drugs for major psychotic disturbance (see, for example, Guimón, 1989). We have to acknowledge that general ways of thinking also change over time: that the discourse of surface and depth that was so persuasive in the 1960s

and 1970s, and centrally concerned questions of personal auton-
omy and the critique of the nuclear family, has shifted.*

At the same time, Mary Barnes' account of current problems
in mental health care remains timely. She writes as a former
patient, a longstanding consumer of conventional mental hospital
care; she writes, also, as a founder member of a therapeutic
trust which aims to provide a setting in which people who need
to retreat from 'everyday responsibilities' can do so while in
psychotherapy. She is also right to focus on the unavailability
of psychotherapy on the National Health Service (see also Duncan, 1989), and on its inadequate provision outside London. When
Harry Stack Sullivan described the mental hospital as a 'social
system made up of fixed castes . . . autocratically maintained in
conformity to a relatively small number of simple, explicit rules'
(Sullivan, 1953, p. 226), he wrote as a psychiatrist. In *Something
Sacred* Mary Barnes speaks movingly of what she saw as a patient
as the damaging effect of an investment in rules and routine,
of the regulatory aspect of mental hospital.

In addition, her experience raises an important theoretical issue
– that of the place of regression in the treatment of psychosis;
in her framework such an issue is inseparable from her critique
of mental hospital. For Mary speaks of being able to go backwards
in time as a prerequisite for change: 'going back in order to
go forward'. Such a view forms a strong contrast with that repre-
sented in standard textbooks for psychiatrists, psychiatric nurses
and aides, published just before or during the time of Kingsley
Hall (see, for example, Muller, 1962; Robinson, 1964; American
Psychiatric Association, 1969; see also Shader and Jackson,

---

* See, for example, Juliet Mitchell's very significant commentary
on Laing's thought and the post-war period (Mitchell, 1974), which
unpacked Laing's use of the experience/behaviour distinction; and Marike Finlay's reflections on post-modern theorists of language: 'The surface of the sign is the only reality to which the sign refers' (Finlay,
1989, p. 50). For a psychiatric perspective on changing attitudes in
the United States to family intervention, see Harvard Medical School
(1989).

1981). They acknowledge the impulse towards regression in mental disorders, but see it as something not to be fostered, even when regression is acknowledged as providing release from adult responsibilities and described in a sympathetic way. Or take the view, put forward by an intelligent and sensitive commentator on Laing: 'Our goal is to set up an institution in which regression is not fostered and yet which can be a retreat' (Lidz, 1972, p. 125). Mary's experience, by contrast, speaks of regression as the key moment, the axis, in a reintegration of self. In the first book we see the project of a regression left to follow its own course, in action; in the second we see Mary's thoughts about it: on the importance of not getting stuck in a regression; of its not being unduly indulged in; its different course in each individual; the part it has to play in healing.

Readers of *Something Sacred* will be able to judge for themselves whether such a view of regression and its therapeutic potential provides its own justification. I want, lastly, to come back to the question I raised at the beginning of this introduction about the fascination that Mary Barnes' experience has aroused. I think the experience may be fascinating because of the way in which Mary transgressed a taboo, and the way in which that transgression was met. Although there are hints, in *Mary Barnes*, of incestuous transgression in the Barnes family, the sustained transgression concerns shit. Working in a mental hospital one is aware of how common it is for certain kinds of psychotics to smear shit, or use it to frighten, or to rebel, or to hope for help. By the same token, as Schwartz and Stanton noted in a perceptive study (Schwartz and Stanton, 1950), such a process is taking place in a Western culture which treats incontinence in adults as highly unacceptable. 'How vital in every society', Lidz puts it, 'are the taboos placed upon things that force the self to conceive what is not-self. In the way we teach children to look at their faeces, for instance, we have the establishment of ego boundaries' (Lidz, 1972, p. 136). The resonance of such an observation for an understanding of Mary Barnes' life over a number of years is, I think, clear: Mary chose not to regard her shit as separate from herself, as something to be removed, but as something to 'stay with', to use therapeutically within rather than against her relationships with those around her. In so doing she did 'give up' her ego boundaries. What she did remained a profound transgression of a cultural norm; but one could continue from there to suggest that the transgression was in the name of a felt necessity. Here, then, is a challenge to mental hospital practice which remains thought provoking: the extent to which conventionally accepted patterns of everyday life need to be given up, in certain disordered states, before healing and recovery can begin. The original response to the book and the play about Mary's life shows us something of the interest which the wider public takes in such matters.

Boston, Massachusetts
AUGUST, 1989

Acknowledgements
In London, my thanks to Fran Acheson; also to Diane Waller and Joan Woddis of the British Association of Art Therapists, and to Julia Vellacott, for helpful conversations about the context of *Mary Barnes*. In Boston, where I have been working on the acute unit of a state mental hospital, I am grateful for discussions with Morris Schwartz, which helped me to formulate my introduction; to Deborah Oliveira who typed the bibliography; and especially to my aunt, Hilda Scott, for her sustained involvement with the project. Throughout, I should like to thank the staff of Free Association Books for their assistance, especially Selina O'Grady for her editorial acumen, and Simona Sideri for transcribing the tapes.

R. D. Laing died in August 1989 while this book was in production.

PART 1
Conversations

1

REFLECTIONS ON *Mary Barnes: Two Accounts of a Journey Through Madness* AND ON KINGSLEY HALL

Ann Scott (AS): I want to begin by asking you to reflect back on the book; to tell me something about how it came to be written.

Mary Barnes (MB): It came because Joe – Dr Joseph Berke – asked me, as I had had a very long and deep experience in Kingsley Hall, if I would write a book with him on my experiences of my time there and of my earlier times too, especially of my childhood.

AS: Would you have had the idea yourself?

MB: I might have, although before Kingsley Hall, the only writing that I had ever had published were professional nursing articles in the *Nursing Times*. But I had tried to write poetry as a teenager; and looking back I think if I'd had more opportunity and perhaps sought expert advice on what I was really suitable for, I think it's *just* possible I might have got into journalism rather than nursing.

I had no idea of my artistic ability in those days, and I think I would have been very afraid to compete with my mother, who did delicate water colour paintings and could also write poetry. I felt very overshadowed by her, and in any case, when I tried to write poetry I felt it was something almost wicked. I hid it away and I would never have admitted to it; so in the circumstances I think probably, not wanting to go into an office or shop,

I did the best I could. I wanted to get away from home and I went into nursing.

Only much, much later, thanks to Dr R. D. Laing and Dr Joseph Berke, did I come to be able to use my real underlying gifts. My life was so radically changed that I think I would have wanted to tell people about it, so it's just possible that I might have written about it. But without the help of Dr Joseph Berke and the support of Dr R. D. Laing, whether it would ever have seen the light of day is very debatable. It gave me great encouragement and personal satisfaction to be involved in the way that I was, rather than have doctors write medical articles about me in medical publications.

The book was written with the very conscious idea that it should be acceptable to professional people – doctors, social workers, psychologists – but that it should also be readable by the general public.

AS: The idea that there would be two accounts, one by you and one by Joe Berke, was worked out in advance?

MB: Yes, I think from the beginning it was envisaged by Joe Berke that we should, between us, write a book, and I from the beginning agreed with this. I wrote my part first, it went through several drafts, and then Joe wrote his account.

AS: How did you find the writing went?

MB: I think at first it was rather tight. Joe and Michael Dempsey, who was then our editor [at MacGibbon & Kee], helped me to write more freely, so for me it went through six drafts, eventually: I wrote and wrote and wrote. And then we cut it. But I think my recall was very clear, and that was because I had been just involved with myself in Kingsley Hall; Joe had had to go out and find himself work in London as a psychotherapist, apart from living in Kingsley Hall. Also, I was not holding on, as Joe was in his situation, so much to a professional attitude.

AS: Let me ask about the reception of the book. I remember, when it came out in the seventies, how much of an impact it made. It made a great impact on me, and most people whom I knew read it. It was translated into seventeen languages. Can you tell me something about how the book was received and what new things it brought to your life, as it became widely known?

MB: In a certain way I felt very close to a lot of people that I knew I would probably never meet in the flesh; many people wrote to me, from abroad as well as in this country. In some ways it made the world seem very small.

I remember I was in the attic in North London, where I was living before the book came out, and I was feeling, as it were, separate from the world, but not in a bad way. I felt very full of love, very good. I was rather fasting and not going out and Joe was coming to me; but it was a very good withdrawal, I was not regressed – I fed myself. My body was very very hot, and I had to use cold water to lessen the burning heat of my body at night so I could sleep. But I had no fever, I was not physically ill.

AS: Bad for you is always associated with feeling angry.

MB: Yes, and having difficulty in laying still with myself; having not-positive thoughts, as it were . . .

AS: Destructive thoughts.

MB: Right, exactly. Well I didn't have those and I remember, as it got nearer to the time for the book to come out, I was gradually coming up and out. There was a lot of publicity; I did a lot of television and radio. I remember Joe used to say, 'See if they will let you read one of your own stories.' I didn't often get the chance but when I did I liked to do this. I do remember one thing that did sometimes affect me bodily: walking along the road I would sometimes feel that my body was going to come apart. Joe used to say to me, 'Oh, ask them to send a taxi or come for you in a car if you're going to a studio to do television or radio.' So I did and I found this a great help.

I was very excited, of course, when the Claude Gill exhibition happened when the book officially came out.* I was also very happy, I enjoyed it very much. It was a very moving experience

---

* 1971

to meet Dr Werner's widow, the widow of the doctor who had got me out of the mental hospital when I was in my late twenties [Barnes and Berke, 1971, pp. 54–5] – and I gave her a painting, one which she liked.

The book, of course, did very deeply affect my life. I felt grateful for that which I had come to: the writing and very much the painting. But I was also aware that the biggest asset to me was the change in my inner emotional feelings: that life was no longer a prison being endured until physical death. I loved the world and I loved life and still do.

At the end of 1971, when I went to take the book to my parents who were then still alive and living near Cape Town, I had a wonderful experience with my mother because I could hold her and embrace her; I no longer had that terrible feeling that I wanted to hit her. I felt a great love and compassion towards my parents because, due to my own experiences, I could see them in a way that I hadn't previously been able to. I had learnt how to accept the gap: that one cannot give to one's nearest and dearest that which one has inwardly received. You have to accept, especially when they are very elderly parents, as mine then were, that what you can verbally say is very limited, but if you can feel love then this is for oneself a very rewarding experience. Also, you are at peace with yourself in that you know you can't talk with them, but you accept that you can, for example, only talk about the weather.

AS: Were you able to talk about the book with them?

MB: Not really.

AS: Would you have wanted to?

MB: No. Only if they had wanted to, which they didn't. The book was put aside but it was not actively criticized and I was accepted in my flesh and blood. I spent a lot of time with them. I hadn't intended to paint but my mother wanted me to finger paint, so I got canvas and paint and did. She came to watch me while I was sitting on the floor doing it. Previously she had said she couldn't understand it and I said, 'Oh mother you *do* paint' – she had her watercolours framed in the lounge. She said, 'Yes my dear, but not like you.' When she said, 'not like you', she said it in a very nice way, giving me credit.

AS: One of your anxieties having always been that you would be competing with her, and indeed would surpass her.

MB: That's right. She saw something in it. The only conversation, really, was when I tried to reassure her that it was not necessary to have regrets that she hadn't helped me, for example, to go to an art school. If that had happened I would have painted; but it would not have had the power that she was recognizing in it, if I'd come to it in a more usual manner.

She had herself learnt in a more technical manner. I realized that what I liked most about her painting was when she was, for example, just doing the sea and it became a bit more abstract and free. One seemed to sense something in it, then, that you didn't when it was much more photographic and controlled. I think she felt satisfied that she had seen something of what I was doing. She accepted it and that gave me a lot of satisfaction, as well as her.

Sometimes I worried unduly on that visit, that I might have upset them unnecessarily; I was very aware that I probably wouldn't see them alive again. I remember once I followed my mother into the bedroom – I was going to try and revise something I'd said; nothing of great importance, but maybe something a bit revealing or that might have been unnecessarily hurtful. I wasn't angry – I didn't have anger against them at all – and as I followed her into the bedroom she was drawing the curtains. She smiled very nicely at me, as a kindly old lady [would], and she said [*bright voice*], 'Hello my dear, just routine.' Every night she went in to draw the curtains at that time and I smiled too and participated, as it were, mentally, in her routine. I had no idea of saying what I was going to bring up with her; whatever it was, I've forgotten now.

AS: And that was a solace?

MB: It was! It was a realization to me that she was in her world and it was not for me to try to bring her into mine, but to respect hers and leave it at that. I had learnt, as I say

- 7 -

in my own words, to accept a gap. I've said it to other people as well, when they've been very concerned to churn it over with the parents. I say, 'Accept the gap, see them in their world.' You appreciate then what their life has been, and how it has been narrowed and limited because they didn't know of other possibilities ... They couldn't ever have what you have had, your chances to expand and live your life. They have done their best in very cramped circumstances, and you're not there to judge whether they did their fullest best with their circumstances or not, but to meet where you can and accept the rest.

I think I'd had a lot of help from Joe before I took the book out to them. I remember it had been a big concern to me that being away from people that knew me – therapists and the more understanding people I knew in England – I might be a bit overcome by isolation and not very good feelings, like guilt, in relation to my parents. He had simply said that if I felt bad I should go to my room and lie down and shut the door until it lifted; and remember that nobody out there would know as much as I knew about myself, never mind any more than me, or be able to help me. In fact I had very few difficult feelings.

AS: So you were able to take him with you internally on that trip.

MB: I think so.

AS: That was family contact and the implications of the book for family relationships. When people wrote to you about the book did their letters, directly or indirectly, show that they wanted something from you as guidance for their own lives? Did you find yourself involved in correspondence about people's mental states? What I'm getting round to is the context of the experiences that led you into your later involvement with other households.

MB: I always felt very much that I wanted to help, to be of some positive use to other people. Sometimes it was just putting them in touch with a person who was practising as a psychotherapist; sometimes it involved putting them in touch with an address for a household or how to find a therapist; it has involved making tapes to send to a blind person in the States – that I still do (she has got a therapist there); but by and large I didn't get into long and lengthy correspondence. The book involved me in many friendships with people who were still quite smashed at times: I didn't so much seek this, but if I felt I could help I didn't want to immediately withdraw and not use my own experience in some way. Joe said the book was a means of hope to many – this I agree with, it has been – but I didn't want people to feel that I was magic in some way. This was my life and my experience; they had their lives, as I had mine. If they tried to be Mary Barnes that was not helping them to be John Smith, or whatever.

AS: Did you ever feel any temptation to *become* magical? The book comes out; it's very widely noticed; you go on television; all kind of things happen in the public sphere. You were in a sense a celebrity.

MB [*laughing*]: In a strange way!

AS: Did you ever find that that became compelling for you, the real Mary Barnes?

MB: Not exactly. I would say more that it became a bit frustrating that I couldn't give them what they were looking for. I had to accept that I'm not God. As I expressed it verbally at times I simply would say, 'I'm not magic.'

AS: That's a very nice way of putting it.

MB: Yes. In Kingsley Hall I was not so aware of this – in fact I very definitely tried to make my brother go my way when he came to live in Kingsley Hall. I tried to *make* him go down.

AS: I was very struck, when you were describing 'accepting the gap' with your parents in South Africa, how different that sounds from your description in the book of wanting Peter to go your way.

MB: Oh yes.

AS: It's also one of the central themes in the play.

MB: It's so valid in more minor ways. [*Voice of mild parody:*] 'Oh Mary paints, if we paint all will be well'; I got the impression some people felt this. 'Oh Mary does sculpture, she makes things with clay, all right if we do clay, sculpture or painting . . .' I didn't exactly, intentionally, keep it absolutely to myself – obviously I didn't, my paintings were all around on paper, on the walls of the Hall. But I was not as aware as I later became of how I must see a person in *their* separate body to me, and as a person with a unique, different life from mine; what was good for me was not necessarily good for them.

This, like a young child, I didn't always realize, in Kingsley Hall times. I think if I wanted to be helpful to someone I'd simply try to make them do what I'd done and everything would be all right. It was almost like saying, 'Joe you've given me a magic sweet, it's helped me, give one to them and they'll be all right.' Well, of course, it is much more involved than giving a pill. What I came to feel was that I'd been given a very special experience that not only brought me to my own life but could give other people an idea that they could become more fully themselves in their own lives, without copying me. But this is a later feeling about the whole thing and something that I've tried to convey to others.

I think that sometimes one does, as when climbing a hill, have a big vision; then you go down through the woods again. You're not meant to wallow in it for the rest of your life, nor can you. But I do think that sometimes you have a glimpse that is sustaining for a long time. This reminds me of a question once on radio or television, when the interviewer said [*mock haughty voice*], 'Well Mary, and are you happy now?' [*laughs*] That is to say, 'after all that'. My reply was that what I felt was rather satisfaction in getting on to my own path in life, which at times involved a joy not hitherto known to me; and was something much deeper than a superficial level of happiness. I hoped I did know what it meant to feel great joy at times, but also I wasn't changed into someone that could never feel misery or despair or suffer. In some ways when you are more fragile and sensitive, you feel more; you feel very intensely; I think any therapist would tell you this. You come to realize, of course, that you still maintain your individuality when you are sharing in something with someone else.

AS: I'm interested in your saying that you weren't changed into someone who couldn't feel despair. There is a sense, I think, in which states that precede certain forms of breakdown could themselves *be* defences against the ordinary human emotions of despair or misery.

MB: Yes, yes, that's right.

AS: It's a very paradoxical situation.

MB: Oh it is, indeed. A polished surface, a veneer that covers over despair. I always think of the contrariness of Christ (or the contradictoriness of emotions), to use an example from my faith.

I think even as a physical nurse, years ago, I had some awareness that in the relief of suffering is involved a participation *in* the suffering, and that sharing sorrow as well as joy is important to us. All through this life we are always alone, but we are also always together.

I do think it's a tragedy when people are so cramped that they can only feel guilt and shame and not joy. My mother suffered like that and I remember saying to her once, 'Oh Mother, Father's talking about going on holiday, you're not going to prison.' Because the reaction was as if she was going to go to prison: she went dead and was very upset because her security was threatened (she was always used to doing the same thing in the same place every day). I realize now that it's what people would call the result of extreme anxiety, but years ago we didn't understand the causes for these things.

AS: And yet it seems to me that in some way you were able to make your peace even with that aspect of her personality, because when you were in South Africa and went into the room where she was pulling the curtains and she said, 'just routine', you had quite an accepting response to it.

MB: Oh yes, I did then; that was after Kingsley Hall, you see. I think I came to be able to see people more where they were and to realize that, unless they wished to change, it was not for me to try to intervene. I think somehow you have to come to a point of really seeking change yourself; very often, if someone is trying to put it onto you and you are not in a suitable state to receive it, it will push you further away from the possibility of it.

AS: The subtitle of your book, *Two Accounts of a Journey Through Madness*, can give the impression of a process which comes to fruition, or comes to an end; of a cycle being completed. Kingsley Hall came to an end in 1970; the lease ran out. Before we talk about where you feel you were in yourself, at the point where Kingsley Hall as a community came to an end, let me ask you to retrace the early days there.

MB: Before I was at Kingsley Hall I was more divided: the intellectual part was split off from the baby part, and my nursing years aided and abetted it. I remember soon after I went to Kingsley Hall – I had been teaching in nursing school not so long before that – Joe once said to me [*stern voice*], 'And don't you give me a lecture'. I had been laying down the law to him about any and every current issue, in a superior manner. I was becoming very baby but I could still be the official tutor; I was used to sitting in an office and having people knock at the door before they came in. (I always tried to help student nurses in a sympathetic way, because I didn't like them being torn to bits by superiors. I wanted to encourage their good feelings and was sympathetic to their unhappiness at times, but I had also been used to maintaining a certain professional standing. It went with the uniform.)

As I got more together I don't think it would have been possible for me to answer Joe back in a way that would suggest I was giving him a lecture, because I became more together and more spontaneous and less intellectual. I remember, when I was first in Kingsley Hall, literally throwing my textbooks across the room because I was so afraid I would get up into my head again if I read them. When I came to use my body more, became able to dance, I used to sing a lot, play ball a lot, and start painting.

Then, looking back, I considered myself much more a real person than when I was in a uniform and seemingly in a superior nursing situation. I never wanted to go back to that sort of nursing situation, *never*, however much I wanted to help people; I never sought to go back into the traditional nursing life, within or without a psychiatric hospital or milieu, because my whole attitude had been so radically changed.

[When the lease ran out] I had lived in Kingsley Hall five years; it was the first time I had lived in any one place for as long as five years since I had been a real, physical child in my parents' home and I was not at all happy about leaving. I felt it was my *home*. In fact, although my paintings were got into store in the warehouse/studio of a friend of Joe's, I was still alone in Kingsley Hall. I hadn't got anywhere to go and I couldn't seem to be quick enough off the mark to follow up the advertisements in the *Evening Standard* to get myself a place. I was always too late, somebody had got there before me.

I was going from Kingsley Hall to Joe once a week for therapy then, to where he lived, and I showed him the paper and he said, 'What's this?' I said, 'I can't afford it,' and he said, 'I think you'd better go up to see about it.' It was the attic that I came to live in in Hampstead . . . [*hesitates*] I was very happy once I got used to living alone. I had never really lived in such circumstances before; I had only known nursing homes and more or less supported housing, in that I had always lived in the army [as a nurse] with other people, in accommodation that was got for me. This was single rented accommodation and I had a lot of my own things there. It was furnished, but I added to it, and I painted there and got used to being there. Like a bird out of a nest I started to fly; I enjoyed it very much.

AS: When you look back on the Kingsley Hall experience – for instance through Joe Berke's account, which gives a description of you as perceived by others – how does that part of the book now strike you?

MB: Well, I remember my own difficulties of course, with regards to the state I was in and what I was going through. How I couldn't come out of it in order to explain it in terms of verbal communication to the other people; and they couldn't have understood it anyway if I had (and talking about something anyway can stop you from going down into it). I wouldn't have wanted to have come out of it in order to try and explain. I can remember feeling very sad at times because, you know, [*laughs*] I so wanted to be popular, to be accepted, and I was going about it in exactly the opposite way.

AS: Joe Berke brings that out in the book, doesn't he?

MB: Yes, he does. I remember that once I was very sad and I said to Joe, 'I don't know, it's not fair, why is it, I'm not throwing crockery about the kitchen, I don't break things, and yet do you know, they don't like me and I want to be liked.' He said, 'Oh Mary your paintings go very deep into people.' I came later to realize that other people were disturbed by things in themselves that *my* behaviour was rapidly bringing up in them. I think they were primarily frightened about things deep in themselves that were expressed as fear of me. They were not all in therapy, not all the time anyway; and when a person is in such a milieu and is resistant to having therapy themselves, then it's very frightening to them to see another person in a very raw, uncovered state.

AS: Were your fellow residents at Kingsley Hall not themselves in therapy, if they were in states of regression or breakdown?

MB: They were in states of breakdown, psychotic states largely, but they were not all in therapy. Nowadays, and certainly in Scotland with the group I've formed, the Shealin Trust, [see below, pp. 33–37], we do ask that people have made a conscious decision not to rely totally on physical treatment and medication; that they have made a conscious choice towards psychotherapy. But this was not so in Kingsley Hall with everybody that came *after* I was there; some of them were not in therapy or in group therapy – whether they wanted it or not – but they were still living there. It was the sixties; some of them wanted to have a nice hippie time, and it could be quite disruptive. I felt that this could make great problems for people who were very fragile and in therapy, if the fears of the others, who might not be in therapy, caused a lot of resistance in them.

It became very difficult for them [the ones not in therapy] to understand why other people were not actively going out shopping or cleaning the place, though it's not to say that they necessarily did housework themselves or had any expectations put upon them to do it. We didn't even have a rota in Kingsley Hall. Nobody *had* to do anything. With regards to some of the people, they were themselves doing what was really too much for them, but they were not *asked* to do it, and were not in any way *forced* to do it – they chose to do it, perhaps to push down their own feelings. Then they could get quite angry with somebody like me who was sitting about the place and not making any effort.

AS: I think it's always very difficult. I believe certain mental states in others are genuinely very difficult to bear; they may or may not stir up unresolved business of one's own. That is, I think there are behaviours or forms of self-expression which will always be difficult for other people to take, if they transgress (or seem to transgress) boundaries of privacy; areas of emotional discretion, if I can put it like that.

One of the lasting impressions I have from Joe's part of the book is that some of the states that you were in led to ways of being, for you, which were upsetting to others in and of themselves, not just because they stirred up painful things for others. When some of the people in the Hall felt, 'How does she get away with behaving like this?', I wonder how such issues strike you now, now that many years have passed.

MB: Yes. I don't think that I could have gone into my own depths and been encouraged to do what I wanted to do – which I was, of course – if I had stopped to consider their feelings. I couldn't. I would have been in a state of trying to go two ways at once, which you can't really do. In these regressed states you have to come to a point where you are considering yourself rather than the effects of your behaviour upon others; this is left more to the person who's guiding you through it to cope with. All right; there does come a certain point of discipline, where you simply have to hold it and, with the help of the person guiding you, agree to behave in certain ways because you are giving out more than can be taken by other people; so a balance is reached.

But if I had tried to concern myself too much on my own with this, then I don't think I would have gone through my own experience; and I don't think I could have gone through it without the guidance of a therapist, because the force of contrary opinion would have been too much for me.

AS: It's interesting that you say that. I'm wondering about the extent to which this perspective has emerged since the Kingsley Hall period came to an end. The book itself ends with a sense of an unfinished story; the way you're talking about Kingsley Hall now suggests that you've had many years to reflect on the necessary stages that one goes through. There is initially a period of utter self-absorption –

MB: There is, yes.

AS: And then a period of being able to give out as much as one's taken.

MB: Yes. As Joe once said, 'The more you can receive, the more you will give.' I'm also very aware that in the receiving there is also a giving, and in the giving there is a receiving. Joe brings this out most clearly in the video [see below, pp. 24–5] where he says it [Kingsley Hall] was the right thing, the right time for him; that I helped him to maintain his inner dialogue with himself [see also Barnes and Berke, 1971, p. 237]. I think that although it's not usually verbally acknowledged by people in the so-called helping situation, this always goes on in any analytic situation. The giving from the one who is most down is, of course, of a non-verbal nature.

I think I must have had an influence – even if I didn't see anybody for two or three days when I was away in a room – on other things that were going on in the building. Looking back, I think that I myself couldn't possibly have consciously stopped what was happening around the time of my paintings coming down.* But I think if you could, as it were, have two feet in two worlds at the same time you wouldn't really have run the most *terrible* risks that I ran at that time of being put away in a mental hospital. But I was behaving in a spontaneous manner: I don't think I could have seen the thing in any way sufficiently from both sides. It was a matter of trust, you see, in the way that Joe had my trust enough so that I had some sense of obedience and of being guided; but it *is* very difficult. I have known similar things, not to quite such a big degree, with other people since in households.

AS: Could you say a bit about that?

MB: Well, yes. For example, after Kingsley Hall and after my time of living in North London I came to live again in Archway [see below, pp. 21–2]; there was a psychology student there who went into regression and was very very frightened. I was trying to help him in ways of bathing and feeding, and I remember he had a chamber pot. If ever that appeared outside his room some people could get very upset. They were frightened that Roger would behave in a manner that would not be acceptable, or that he'd get violent. One inevitably becomes involved in that, if one is seen as the helping figure to that person. (Roger actually nearly left the house once, but he was fortunately saved by another man that went with him; he had allowed another man to go with him. He was got back into the house during the night.)

It's practically impossible, if you're the one that's really down and being helped, to understand the extent of the anxiety you're

---

* As Mary's 'flow of paintings' increased and 'more and more of her work got plastered about', tension rose at Kingsley Hall. One group of residents felt she was trying to engulf and control the community, another that she was embarked on a spiritual journey. Eventually a majority decision was reached that the paintings should come down. At this time there was also a question, in the minds of some, about Mary's continued residence at Kingsley Hall, but the crisis was resolved and Mary stayed there. For Mary Barnes' account, see Barnes and Berke, 1971, pp. 172–6; for Joe Berke's, see Barnes and Berke, pp. 264–8. Quotations in this note are from p. 265. [*AS*]

provoking in your fellow residents, and to stop to consider what you're doing and how you're putting yourself in danger because they're getting so frightened they can't bear you in the place. Apart from the fact that your paintings are frightening them because they're all around the walls; apart from the fact that you're not coming to meals, they get frightened because you're away in your room all the time.

AS: And they experience that as a rejection, at some level?

MB: I think they must have done. Yes, you might reply, like I used to: 'Well Joe, I'm not stopping *them* putting paintings on walls, they can stay in *their* rooms if they want to all day.' But this was not how they saw it, and you need somebody who sees both sides of the thing; who understands the balance that *must* happen in such a group, no matter what extremes the person that's down is in, when, as it were, the edge is reached . . .

AS: Of what becomes oppressive to others, unacceptable to others.

MB: Yes, it must be dealt with. For example, Paul [Zeal] would take me out of my room and sit me at the kitchen table when somebody got very worried because I wasn't eating. You might say, 'Why aren't they in their room and going into their own thing?' – the resident was not functioning as a therapist as such, and resistance might take the form of psychological discussions around the kitchen table. And sometimes it's a false defence against their feelings, to get over-worried about another person who is in good hands anyway and is not their direct responsibility; but sometimes they feel like that and the balance of the group has to be dealt with. Perhaps it's a bit like being a parent when one of your children, the youngest, is having a lot of help and is sick, and the older one gets very frightened and worried. It's a very tricky situation to deal with; to be able to recognize the fear that's being aroused in the more 'up' person. Also, you want to encourage the person who's doing what they want – who's lying in a room and 'not doing' – to continue like that, if it seems right for that other person.

I think on the whole it was very skilfully managed in Kingsley Hall; and somehow, by the grace of God, I managed to just about toe the line when it was vital that I needed to [*laughs*], so that I could stay there.

AS: How do you feel now about Joe using a word like 'manipulative' to describe you? One way or another it is a recurring theme of his part of the account. 'Mary tried to manipulate her environment (by regression) so that she was taken care of in a way which could be identified with an intra-uterine existence' [Barnes and Berke, 1971, p. 375; see also p. 242].

MB: Yes. I think that anybody who is really regressed, without consciously thinking the thing out, is like the baby in a household . . .

AS: Controlling things?

MB: Terribly, yes! That's how they felt the baby behaviour was, a very controlling factor.

I think it's very difficult for a parent figure – for anybody, really – to love without possession; I think that's a lot of what it's about. We all tend to put strings onto our love and the more free one becomes the more possibility there is, really, to love without possession, without strings. We do in life, in general, tend to manipulate each other. But I think the more you are truly trying to live your own life, the less likelihood there is of doing it.

But the baby unconsciously does it, and the ways of dealing with this used to be much more rigid than they are today. In my parents' generation, with regard to feeding, it was thought very bad to give in to a child screaming for its mother's milk. It must scream until the exact hour of the feed was due. Nowadays there is much more to be said for feeding on demand; but, of course, one recognizes the mother has her life and she must have a rest now and again from the baby sucking the breast. Babies are like a person who is really very regressed. They can't exactly see it from that angle, so a firm limit has to be laid down, and even if it's painful for the child, or the subject who is regressed, then it has to be enforced. Because if the person who is the caring figure, the parental figure, allows themselves to be too much the doormat, to be sucked dry, then that's very bad for them. It will lead to repressed anger in them which, even if they don't verbalize it, will have a very bad effect on the person closest to them.

AS: I agree.

MB: And we are all only human.

MAY 1988

2

1971–1988
AND THE WORK OF
THE SHEALIN TRUST

AS: When we talked the last time, you had left Kingsley Hall, the lease having run out, and Kingsley Hall had closed as a community. A year later your book was published. I know that in the early 1970s you went to live in The Archway, a household in North London. Tell me something about that.

MB: That was a household of two neighbouring houses. Ronnie Laing was a bit involved with Archway at the time, because it was only the second lot of housing that the Philadelphia Association (PA) had got since Kingsley Hall: Leon Redler had got a little house that was condemned to carry on Kingsley Hall work, and when that was eventually going to be bashed down the local authority gave them these two houses in the Archway area of London. It was at this time, when there was more space again in the housing, that I felt I wanted to go back into it, but this time I more or less had to move anyway because the attic hadn't got a proper fire escape.

When I first went there I rather withdrew myself, and someone used to visit me to bring me food, a young American psychology student by the name of Roger. Later on Roger lived in the front half of a long room that opened at the back on to the garden; I was in the other half, but without fully realizing what was happening with Roger inside himself.

I remember that he got up from where he was lying on the

floor and knelt over me and said, 'I don't know that I want you here.' I kept silent and he went and lay down again. After some time, probably a week or two, he found it emotionally increasingly difficult to leave his own space, to go upstairs to the toilet or out to the kitchen. I felt it was too much for him and I realized he was regressing. His therapist used to come to visit him; his therapist was not a person of the PA group, actually.

AS: So The Archway included people who had been at Kingsley Hall, and some of the therapists.

MB: Yes. Joe was only involved in so far as he kept some contact with me, but he was not regularly visiting the house because he was starting another group [the Arbours] with Morty [Schatzman]. But I still had hopes that the PA would get a house in the country and that was primarily why I stuck with them: Joe's group only intended to maintain work in London and I wanted to go to the country.

AS: What were the differences between Joe's group and the PA at the time?

MB: Well, I don't know really that there was much difference at the time. But as both groups have developed I think it is true to say, especially as Joe's group has a crisis centre, that his work is a little more structured than the PA work. Some of the therapists who were involved in the original group are now either in Joe's group or with the PA group; and some have left alto- gether. For example, Ronnie Laing isn't involved with either group.

AS: How would you characterize your own state of mind at the time? I ask because one of the enduring images from the book is that the one who is down needs the help of someone who is in a relatively stable phase in order to come up; it sounds as though you were going to be that person for Roger.

MB: Yes, on the whole coming up isn't really a problem. In the case of Roger, he came up very quickly, but I was quite withdrawn at the time I was caring for him. I didn't go out; I didn't dress; on the other hand, I did go outside the room in the house to get water from the kitchen – sometimes to wash

Roger. Eventually he let me help him up the stairs to the bath, as it was too much for him to go up the stairs alone, really – he was very fragile – and I fed him for a time.

Eventually Roger got worried that he might have a physical illness, but he didn't want to be examined by a P A physical doctor; he wanted to go out and I persuaded a friend of his to go with him. He got back in the night to the house and gradually came up after that; there was nothing seriously wrong with his body. I'm happy to say that Roger is now back in the States and is working as a therapist in Philadelphia, and in fact is married to a therapist also. He is very concerned about the lack of adequate housing facilities in the States, as well as over here, for people who need to be in such a milieu when they are going through an acute phase in psychotherapy or may wish to regress.

AS: I was struck last time by your saying that you didn't want people to feel that you were magic; I was wondering whether when you were in the Archway household people were in some way responding to you as though you were?

MB: I think not then. As I say, I was a bit withdrawn in caring for Roger; more so than the rest of the other people there, for some of the time; I wasn't going out so much . . .

AS: Maybe that came later?

MB: I think it did, it came later when I was up and around.

AS: Next Dr Laing wanted to establish a psychotherapy household in the country.

MB: That's right. Ronnie had by this time got, with his family, a holiday house in the West Country, near the village of Chagford, just below Dartmoor in Devonshire. I still had a desire myself to go to the country, so I went down a few times to look for somewhere to live. Eventually I found a very tumbledown place that hadn't been lived in for a long time, actually in the village of Chagford.

Thanks to the help of an architect the local authorities decided that although the place hadn't been lived in for some years I could stay there. Very gradually I started towards getting it into a more reasonable place of habitation. In the beginning I had no inside water. There was no electricity and the only heating was from an open fire, but the chimney smoked so badly it was a bit of a problem; I was rather kippered if I put the fire on! I took down the ceiling so it was rather cold in the winter, though it looked very nice with the joists showing. Also I scraped off the plaster from the walls to expose the great lumps of Dartmoor granite. Having only candle light it was for a time like living in a cave [*laughs*], and I enjoyed it; I was so thrilled to be in the country at last.

AS: Then around 1976 a Swedish television film was made.

MB: That's right. The book had been translated into Swedish and Gerard Röhl, who then worked for Swedish television, came over with his crew. He met Joe in London and came to Chagford, and they filmed me finger painting in the cottage. Then we all went to a now empty and fast becoming really derelict Kingsley Hall to finish making this film.

AS: It was the first time you'd been back to Kingsley Hall for five or six years. When I saw the film, I couldn't help wondering how it struck you after that amount of time.

MB: I think I must have felt very much that I was going back home because, when I first saw this film, I was very aware that my speech was much better in Kingsley Hall. If you notice, when I'm answering Gerard's questions in Chagford in the film, I'm putting on a little bit of an accent, as if I'm a bit foreign or Swedish; but when I'm in Kingsley Hall answering questions, I'd say my speech is more pure. I would say this was because I was feeling more secure in a milieu that I felt very towards [sic] and had known very well.

I think I was a bit dismayed at the state of the building, because it was so terribly vandalized and I was a bit upset to see that the door of my room had gone. (I've seen the building since and it's been done up; this little room where I painted my own door in Kingsley Hall is no longer there, it's all been blocked off.) At the time of the video, the room was still there, but the door had been taken off; it was not vandalized, just entirely removed. I remember that I felt a bit sorry I hadn't taken it with me, with the paintings, but I felt I shouldn't take the door of the room from the building [*laughs*] and I'd left it. (I remember it was Leon Redler who said that I should have taken it.) When I saw this room, without a door at all, I did rather wish I had taken the door: it was painted with a tree, so I've lost track of that now, of course.

Kingsley Hall is now being used according to the original wording of its Trust, for the use of the people of Bow. They've built on a very nice extension with very comfortable chairs, for the elderly people to come and have tea and social activities in. The room where the big painting, *Three Stages of Sacrifice*, was, is used, I think, for children's playgroup; they also do yoga there.

AS: Your big painting is still there?

MB: Oh, I'm sorry, it isn't. Ronnie and Joe tried to get the new authorities at Kingsley Hall to leave the painting on the wall and at the time we thought they were going to renovate it and preserve it. Unfortunately, when I went back to show the present people the video of the Swedish television film, the wall had been painted over. At the time we were making the Swedish television film the painting was still there, although the house was vandalized: now the house is in very good shape with central heating and beautifully decorated; but the painting is not there. Joe was quite angry about it; he's very fond of my painting, as am I of course.

AS: It must have been a very potent experience: to go back to an empty Kingsley Hall, but one that had a large painting of yours on a wall.

MB: Yes. The time we were making the Swedish television film, of course, the painting was still there; and I must have been very reassured, I think, to see it was still there and in quite good shape. I felt that I was going back to a home of my childhood; really, my second childhood. Yes, it was a very moving experience, a very good experience.

I always think when I move – and I've moved quite a few times, physically, since then – that one must always look forward, and of course live in the present; but, just as I hadn't wanted to leave the uterus as a tiny premature baby – there was this awful conflict: wanting to be born and yet clinging back – so I must not unduly cling back to where I've just been. But at this time I'd only been a few years in Devon and my clinging back towards Kingsley Hall would have been much more acute than it could be today, for example.

AS: Were you conscious of that at the time?

MB: Oh, I think I was aware of it. On the positive side – although I'd been sad to leave Kingsley Hall – I had had a very good experience in the attic in North London, and that was followed by going to Archway. Obviously, I missed Hampstead Heath and the good things of the attic and there was a slight clinging back but, again, I had a good experience in the Archway household of being of use to another person. That was something very positive to me. Obviously, I had a lot of fears when it came to the actual moving out of London to the country, and being all those miles away from a therapist and people I'd known since the beginning of Kingsley Hall. That was, at the time, quite a frightening experience, but something that I very much wanted. I did feel very isolated, but I was determined to speak about myself to people if I felt it was necessary.

AS: People you were meeting in Devon wouldn't have known your background or wouldn't have known about Kingsley Hall?

MB: Well, by this time the book had been out a few years. When I first got into Devon, as I say, I was aware of the isolation of being physically many miles from a therapist in London (although I was no longer having individual office therapy from Joe, not for some years then). But I was also so thrilled, at last, to be living in the country that I made new contacts. Because the book was out – and if I knew people had had the book or sometimes if I felt they might have – I sometimes would speak of it. I found I could be open about things and answer questions, and it was not a barrier between me and other people; I think if people had known a little bit, but not enough, they might have feared – and I might have feared that *they* feared – that I was a mad person and not quite one of them. I had a certain desire to merge into the background and to be accepted.

AS: What was your pattern of life when you were in Devon?

MB: I was in Chagford a few years and I was trying to find, literally, an empty house that could be used as a household; and also to interest people to come there from London to start therapy work in Devon, apart from making contacts with the few people that were doing non-residential psychotherapy in Devon. Well, somebody told me of a place, above Seaton in Devon, that had been used for mentally handicapped children and was no longer being so used; except that on the ground floor an old lady lived with two mentally handicapped people, adult in years but like children. I went to see the old lady and she said that she would like the building after her death to be used for another mental purpose, not necessarily mental handicap.

So I moved in upstairs and Paul Zeal of the PA came down to look at it. We did have high hopes about it and eventually a PA doctor moved to Exeter from London. By this time Lucy, a person of Devon who was in breakdown, was living upstairs with me. But when the old lady actually died things had not been got together right legally, and we didn't get the building; I had to move again. I had by this time got all my paintings down from London so it was quite an upheaval.

AS: Where did you move to?

MB: I had by this time been to an International Congress at Leuven in Belgium and I was very interested to join an underwater swimming and diving group of Dr Karel Ringoet in Leuven. So, I went to Belgium for some months. During the period I was doing the underwater swimming and diving I had a very strong invitation to go to Buenos Aires: the play [*Mary Barnes*] was doing well there and they much wanted me to go, but I was involved in the swimming and diving.

AS: Tell me something about that.

MB: I understand there are two ways of doing it: in a group, which was the way I did it; or some therapists have put people individually into a tank of water: it's like an enclosed bath.

They're naked and it's dark, and they come out of it when they want, or they stay a certain time and come out of it. It's to give you in feeling a similar experience as you would have had when you were in the uterus before birth.

I think it does take people very deeply down, without any talking about it. So I think it is a very powerful means of pre-birth therapy. I remember at the time the late Frank Lake* wrote to me when I was in Belgium and said he was so thrilled to hear I was involved in this work. He had done primal therapy by people bending on the floor with pressure from cushions and he felt very strongly that something in the water was the next step forward with this work.

AS: I think you know that Free Association Books is publishing a group of papers from the Philadelphia Association [Cooper and others, 1989]. The book includes an account of the history of the organization, and I learned from it that differing views of birth (and presumably pre-birth) therapy had created 'fundamental tensions' within the network. Some felt that large group 'birthing' events were not a form of therapy in the ordinary sense of the word.

MB: Well, I think I had a good experience of it . . . [*hesitating*] I had already known very early and, in some ways, pre-birth feelings in Kingsley Hall and I consider it a very powerful means of therapy. I remember, before my experience of the underwater swimming and diving, I had been on the floor and had pressure from cushions, particularly at a weekend group when the late Bill Swartley from Canada, the psychologist, had been over. At that weekend group I had asked Bill if he would do this primal therapy on me, and I remember I went up to a bathroom and put my head under the water, and went into the bath so my hair was all dripping wet. I was very wet, I was naked, I started

---

* Trained both as a psychiatrist and a missionary, Frank Lake founded the Clinical Theology Association in the early sixties in an attempt to bring together the insights of theology and pyschology.

to move my body when I felt [I wanted] to and the people above me allowed this and released the pressure of the cushions. As I moved I had very strong feelings of what I imagine must have been birth feelings. As I opened my eyes I saw a squashed grape on the floor. I remember, I picked this up and I thought, 'Yes, I've just about been back there, to the feeling of being a cell.' Although I could cope with the outside, I *was* regressed, I had been and still was when I got up from this position. So it took me back a bit into a regressed state; not an incapable state.

When I got to the house I was staying in, I felt I couldn't open the door to the top of the house. Because of the state of regression I was in I wanted the door opened for me. I tried but I didn't feel I could, somehow, and I sat on the stairs the rest of the night. Jane, the mother, said to me in the morning, 'Oh Mary, why ever didn't you wake me, why ever didn't you shout?' I said I didn't like to, it was very late at night. I said to Jane, 'It's all right, they'd asked me to write it up and I sat on the stairs and wrote it all up, so I haven't wasted my night, and I'm OK.' So I went off back to Devon and quickly came up from what was a very obvious sort of setback to a more regressed state.

Comparatively speaking, it was a very minor period of regression. But afterwards, I felt it had furthered my growth. I don't think it could happen to that extent now, if I did it. But, you see, I was not so firmly together in those years – although I could cope very well in Devon – as I am in the 80s, if you understand me.

AS: There must be something that you feel underwater swimming and diving can gain access to, that other forms of therapy cannot.

MB: Yes Ann, I really do think that. I'm sorry to say that I can't read, because it's in Flemish, Karel Ringoet's book, *Was Plato Schizofreen?* But I think Karel Ringoet has done a lot of people a lot of good through this work, by keeping them moving and in an 'outside' way of life after they've had brief experiences in a group which was partly organized by a team of very dedicated professional divers as well as by Karel himself. When I came back to London, Ronnie was looking around to see if we had divers in London to try and do something over here, but it never got off the ground.

Like all work it's selective: one thing is good at one time for a particular person, and it depends on the therapist who is primarily guiding this person at that time, whether they do it or not. Most of all, over and above that, of course, it depends on the desires in the individual person. But I certainly feel that if a person is taken back and has those feelings, even if they don't talk about it, it can be a very powerful part of their therapy. I think many analysts would tell you that people lying on the couch may go through something where their pulse and their breathing are affected; they are going through, with the therapist's help, a sort of birth experience.

AS: Certainly a very early experience, if not a birth experience; certainly an experience before words.

A painful experience came next: the death of your brother. Tell me something about that.

MB: I was often very aware of Peter's isolation and continued suffering in a rather dead way; not only during Kingsley Hall, from which he did benefit, but afterwards. His situation then was that he was living in a men's hostel and working alongside physically disabled people in Remploy in the Holloway area of London. He always looked all right – when I say looked all right I mean that he was smartly dressed, everything without a crease, and a tie on – but underneath I used to feel that he was not really alive; he was withdrawn. I always appreciated how the people in Remploy would let me sit with him in the canteen if I would visit.

If you would have asked me then, 'Do you worry about your brother?' – because I was in Devon and he was in London – I would have said, 'Well, no, I'm sad that he hasn't really been able to come to his own life, but I'm relieved that he's able to basically look after himself physically and that he's got some employment; because it's been his desire to feel he was working in some way and also because it's sheltered employment. He's not under the stress and strain that he would be in an ordinary factory or office.'

But I was always aware that, when I left Remploy and went wherever I was staying that night in London, I felt relief; so I suppose, more than I really realized, I did worry a bit about him. (I often came to London and sometimes I would stay a night or two in the very first crisis centre that Joe got, in Willesden.) I would tell him where I was staying and invite him to come round to see me, before I went back to Devon. Of course, I invited him to Devon, but he never really felt secure enough to go further than about half an hour's walk from where he lived, so he never made it there.

I had known, through my painting, one of the therapists at the crisis centre, because she was from Italy and I'd had an exhibition in Milan and she was aware of me. This was the beginning of my friendship with Andrea Sabbadini and his wife Laura, who were the resident therapists at that time. So I gradually renewed a contact with the Arbours group; I had never completely lost it, but it was more strongly renewed then.

I was still in the flat in Devon, when Peter died after a sudden coronary; Ronnie Laing was in the States; Joe was around and so was Leon Redler. The hostel was in Kentish Town, so I arranged for the Requiem Mass for Peter to be in a church in Kentish Town. I was very gratified to see so many people, from where he worked and from where he lived, come to the funeral; Joe and Leon were there, and people who knew us both when we were children, and it was a very beautiful service. Peter was cremated; he had left a note, written only three weeks before he died, that he wished to be. So, of course, I saw to that and gave flowers on behalf of my sisters (one was in Australia and one was in South Africa) since Peter had died very very suddenly after only three hours in hospital.

Just at that point, the PA doctor in Exeter wondered whether he would be able to get a household going, and for a time I came back to a small household of the PA in Ealing, where there happened to be a place at the time. I was there some months and it was then, around 1984, that I first went to Sweden and met the girl that I still visit in a mental hospital near Stockholm.

AS: Had this first trip to Sweden been connected to the earlier film?

MB: Not directly so, no. The connection was a friend of a Norwegian psychology writer who had once visited me in Devon. Her [Swedish] friend worked mainly with autistic children, but had seen this video and had met me. She wondered if, at the joint invitation of the autistic group and the Art Therapists' Group in Stockholm, I would go and talk. She got a copy of the Swedish television film, and Gerard Röhl came to see it. When we showed it and I talked, a doctor asked some questions and an elderly gentleman did also. I realized later that the elderly gentleman, who asked about how aggression was dealt with in PA households, was the father of the girl in the hospital whom the doctor asked me to visit [see below, pp. 48–9].

Then, Dr Laing, who, as you know, is originally from Glasgow, had ideas of forming something in Scotland and getting a household going up there; I think at that time he was just about stepping out of the PA. An American psychologist and I went up, and somebody who had been connected with the PA also. We tried but nothing really got off the ground. The psychologist went back to the States and then Dr Laing seemed to get settled in the States, especially after his mother died. I came back south, really with the idea of finding somewhere for myself to live [see also below, pp. 51–2].

This would have been 1985–6 time and I had paintings left in the village of Falkland in Scotland, for reasons of my personal contacts there. I was asked to move my paintings because the National Trust needed the space they were in, so I started to look for somewhere for myself. I decided I would try again to form a group in Glasgow for the purpose of getting a residential therapy house. Why Glasgow? Because I seem to know more people in that area who are interested in psychotherapy and quite a few people there are functioning as psychotherapists.

This group has now become the Shealin Trust* and we really hope to get a therapy household going. The director of the Glasgow Association for Mental Health would very much like us to. It helped the whole project on a lot by Dr Joseph Berke coming up to talk in Glasgow in May 1988. It will be something separate, and particular to Scotland, but the Arbours are being quite helpful with regards to getting us off the ground and inviting people to visit the Arbours household in London who haven't had much experience of such things.

AS: What kind of background do they have?

MB: The honorary secretary of the Shealin Trust, Irene Richardson, trained as a psychotherapist with the Arbours Group in London; her friend is from the States and is training as a therapist in Glasgow; another person is from a social work background, but he's done a lot of voluntary work for the Richmond Fellowship.†

I thought, although there is a Richmond Fellowship house in Glasgow, there was a need for a place for people who had chosen to have psychotherapy rather than total reliance on physical treatment, medication. They could live in the security of a comparatively understanding group. The house would have psychotherapists going in to meet with the group and a place where their own individual therapists could take them through some regression, if the therapist and the person concerned wanted it.

By and large, as I see it, people living in the Glasgow household, which will only initially be for about six or seven people, will

---

* The Shealin Trust was started in Glasgow in 1987. Its name was taken from the Scottish word meaning a shelter for shepherds and sheep.

† A network of therapeutic communities for adults and children who are emotionally disturbed or who have had a mental breakdown. It comprises a college, which provides in-service training for Fellowship staff and other professionals in the caring services, and further offers a consultative service. The Fellowship was begun in 1939.

be going out to their individual therapists and there may never be somebody in bed in a room there. But I would feel that in bringing about the household I would have been part of a means of providing a suitable environment for a person to have more help from therapy than they could in more ordinary living situations. For example, some people are very afraid to be alone in a bedsit when they are going through a psychotherapeutic analytical situation; some people would not wish to be living with their own blood family during such a time; many would certainly not want to go into a mental hospital, and a mental hospital is not geared to particularly help people who have chosen to rely mainly on psychotherapy for their means of healing. From the therapist's point of view it would make more possible, with individual clients, than could be achieved in a more ordinary living situation.

The person would have their own room and nobody would question if they didn't go out for some days or if they were always out. There would be no question of them not having their own door key, and they could get up at seven o'clock or eleven o'clock, or at seven in the evening. Many people might tell me they could have this in any ordinary living situation, but in point of fact it isn't true: people, especially living with their own blood family, have an expectation put upon them, that they will get up at a certain time and attend meals. Certainly in any institutional environment this would be anticipated.

It seems very sad to me that people going into mental hospitals are expected to put on their clothes and attend meals and this function and that function when, if they were living alone at home and felt under the weather, they probably wouldn't bother to dress. I always found [when I was] a bit regressed that dressing and undressing was very difficult work. Many people coming into a household find it very difficult either to take off their clothes at night – nobody would have minded in a household if they kept their clothes on all night or what they wear – others like me would not have wanted to put any clothes on [*laughs*].

I think that one's natural inclinations when one is feeling under the weather are, by and large, helpful. A household relying on psychotherapeutic means is, to my way of thinking, more truly a hospital, a place of healing, asylum, refuge, than a state hospital could ever be.

I do think that it does make an awful lot of difference, even if the person is not going through a very deep and long regression of the kind that I went through, if they can have a suitable place to stay. I have admiration for Elly Jansen, the founder of the Richmond Fellowship households, but those households are specifically for people to be helped out of the hospital back into a working situation. Now, if you have a psychotherapeutic household, then going into a working situation is up to the individual, when and if they want it. It's not [a matter of] a positive push from the therapist's side to get out and get on; in fact they are given the opportunity to lie down and 'get in', *if they want*, and that's very important. I have become more and more able, I think, to respect a person's own wishes about that.

AS: So your main reference point in this work is Arbours?

MB: Exactly. But just as the PA are very glad to use an Arbours room and the Arbours are glad to use a PA room, amongst the two groups I feel there is increasing co-operation, and possibly in the future people may be interested to come to see what we have up here.

But as Joe said, the work as a whole needs to spread out up into the Midlands and the North, and I think it doesn't really matter how many particular groups there are. I can see a lot of good in that, because local people are much more inclined to support local projects, especially materially, than something that is two or three hundred or five hundred miles away.

AS: How did you go about making the existence of the Shealin Trust known in the Glasgow area?

MB: Well, I visited a lot of people doing non-residential psychotherapy, so there was quite a big network. In particular, I met two people – a man and his wife – who already felt they would like the use of a house for some of their clients. They have a group called Person Centred Therapy and they recently got an office where they see people. Then I met one or two other people, within the health service actually, and went to talk to them; and I made contact with the Davidson Clinic,* an established clinic that does non-residential psychotherapy. They would like us to have a house and they would send people there, if they felt it was relevant and useful for the individual person, but I've got nobody from there actually involved at the moment. It's like a lot of things: when it happens they feel well able to make use of it, but they're very busy and they don't feel they would like to come to regular meetings.

I decided we needed a very small active group to really get it off the ground and this is what we have. The hereditary keeper in Falkland Palace, who is a social worker by profession, has a lot of legal and business knowledge and he is making sure our constitution is in accordance with Scottish law and consulting various authorities about that.

AS: What does the constitution of the Trust stipulate?

MB: We are there to provide an alternative living situation for people who have made a conscious choice of not relying in breakdown solely on physical treatment through medication; in other words, people who are in psychotherapy.

AS: Is the model for it the Arbours Crisis Centre?

MB: Yes and no. No in that we would not reckon to have people in very severe acute states as Arbours do, because we would not have a resident therapist there. But I do think it would be more like a long-stay Arbours house.

AS: Arbours has social service funding, doesn't it, for individual residents?

MB: Yes, but it has to go through the authorities of the area from where they come; some authorities will give a grant and some won't. I do think that in some cases people have been

---

* It was founded in 1939 by Dr Winifred Rushford to provide psychoanalysis at a moderate cost for the people of Edinburgh.

able to get individual sponsorship from an industrial firm or business firm; I think this is something that needs to be further explored. More than private individuals, organizations and industrial enterprises might be persuaded to give money for a few months for somebody to stay in a crisis centre.

But immediately, what we want to start in Scotland is something in the nature of a long stay household; a house that is probably provided by a housing association. The rent would be obtained from social security and your invalidity or sickness benefit, and the amount of the rent would only be assessed after the people starting the house had been to the DHSS [Department of Health and Social Security] and seen how much the DHSS were prepared to pay them individually, then the rent would be assessed so the individual people, who would be responsible for paying their own rent, would have enough left every week to have money to spend. Hopefully, like the Arbours Association, people might be able to get enough money from the DHSS so that some of it could be used for therapy. We would hope to be able to get this in time.

AS: I was going to ask what provisions you anticipate for residents who might perhaps unexpectedly develop an acute crisis?

MB: It would depend really on their individual therapists, whether they would be prepared to go into the household for longer periods to help them to get through it and on whether they could help other people living in the house to understand enough to help care for them. It's not all that usual for people in long stay houses to go into these acute crisis states, but I feel that in such a house there would be much more opportunity for the therapist, anyway, and the client, to go through a deeper state of therapy than could be possible in a not so favourable living situation. But this would be something between the individual person and the individual therapist concerned, who would be mainly responsible. I would like to think that we could know enough about local hospital facilities that we could have in mind, if necessary, the best sort of place to send a person, because some are better than others.

AS: Of course. So the work of the Shealin Trust is really what preoccupies you most at the moment.

MB: That and responding to any invitation that may come along, to go and give a talk somewhere. When I'm at home I spend quite a bit of time doing painting – I do a lot of finger painting still – and quite a bit answering letters. I don't like to think it's piling up on me, so I do often have to spend an hour or two dealing with the mail and when I come back I always like to get through it and get on.

AS: People write to you about all manner of things?

MB: Yes, even today people will suddenly write and say they've read the book, if they hadn't seen it before, and ask me lots of questions. Sometimes I get an awful lot of writing from people individually, particularly here [the UK] and in the States. They may already have a therapist or they may not, and if they haven't and I know of anyone near where they live then I can suggest it in replying to the letter; but I don't get individually involved with them beyond that, because I think they need somebody to hand.

I just want to reassure them that it's right for them to look for themselves for therapists and that they're not a copperplate copy of me exactly. I'm glad they've read the book, I'm glad they liked it, but they must find a therapist or encourage [their friend] – if it's a friend of somebody who is asking help for someone – to look wherever they live.

AS: From the way that you talk it sounds as though you've gained a fair bit of detachment from that book.

MB: Yes, I think I have. In the first few years after the book was out, I was still a bit as I was with my brother in Kingsley Hall – 'I went down, Peter you must go down' – and I would have tended to think everybody must go to Ronnie or Joe, as if there wasn't another therapist in the world! But now I have a much wider appreciation of things, and I also think for the same person different people and different things can be relevant at different times of their lives. You can never exactly know another person's past; you have to be true to yourself.

– 38 –

AS: What do you think brought you to that realization . . . that people wouldn't necessarily want to go your way, although you had had a period of feeling that they should?

MB: Well, perhaps in some small way, every time I saw the play. I could see so clearly how one-sided I was in my attitude to my brother [*laughs*]. I could see how necessary it is to have more of an objective view and not to think that everybody is just like you.

I also think that travelling has helped me to understand that people will have different ways of being helped, and that applies to any particular aspect of life; there is never only one way. I think it is what you might call providence, really; how the person manages to find the right person or the right way for them at the right time. I think all of us have a certain bit of trueness that seeks its own fulfilment, however messed-up we may have been emotionally or however bad the breakdown is. Through the very particular help I had, I think I have an intense awareness of this. As when I paint I don't always know exactly what I'm doing or how it's going to come; I feel that I live more and more as I paint.

MAY 1988

3

HOUSEHOLDS, HELPING
AND REGRESSION

AS: We've been talking about your recent experience with households; I know from the acknowledgements in your book that
you had many contacts with the Tavistock Clinic in London at
an early stage. How did that come about?

MB: It was initially due to my looking at the time, in 1963,
for somewhere for my brother and I to be together with other
people. He wanted to live alone with me in a flat. I told Peter
of my experiences of breakdown and said that I felt that we could
be together if we were in a group with other people. So I was
seeking, at that time, not only a psychotherapist for myself, and
I had hoped by then for Peter also, but for somewhere where
we could both live with other people.

I had been teaching previously in the Hospital of St John and
St Elizabeth in London, where I was principal tutor. To help
the student nurses in their psychology studies I had considered
it very important to help them to help the mother who would
be in hospital with a sick child. My means of showing the goodness
of this was to show them the two films made by James Robertson,
who worked with John Bowlby in the Tavistock Child Development Research Unit. I used to show these films, *A Two-year-old
Goes to Hospital* and *Going to Hospital with Mother*. They are
a very powerful means of teaching which approach is to be

preferred: which, without doubt, *is Going to Hospital with Mother.** I met James Robertson through these two films and I remember taking him round the hospital of St John and St Elizabeth on one occasion; we were especially delighted to meet Sister Melitus, who was the surgical ward sister. She was always very helpful in teaching the student nurses; I liked her and James talked to her.

Anyway, at this time I also was sometimes able, thanks to James Robertson and John Bowlby, to take the student nurses down to sessions that John Bowlby held at the local child welfare clinic for mothers with their babies. This also was very helpful for me and the student nurses. I think it was James Robertson who introduced me to the work of Isabel Menzies (1959), and I was very interested to read her work about anxiety in student nurses. I had often felt that they had tremendous emotional pressures upon them as very young people, with regard to experiences of other people in great pain, and of people dying and being born. I felt that they needed a lot more understanding and appreciation and love and help themselves, in order that they could help their patients.

AS: When we were talking earlier about your professional experiences, I couldn't help asking myself whether you knew Isabel Menzies' work. Did you ever meet her?

MB: Yes, I did, I met her at the Tavistock Institute for Human Relations and it was a tremendous moral support to me, because I often felt very fragile and in such sympathy with student nurses, especially if they came before me in tears, and there seemed so little that I could do. Nowadays I realize, of course, that simply letting them cry and listening to all their troubles could have been of some help to them, though the only real advice I remember I ever gave them was, 'Try to stick it out because you want your examinations and then, when you are in this situation of

---

* *A Two-year-old Goes to Hospital* shows the rapid psychological deterioration of a small child separated from her mother during hospitalization for a minor operation (see Robertson, J. and J., 1989). [*AS*]

superiority, do not do unto others as was done unto you.' Which I appreciate is very difficult. Of course, I had contact with the sisters and would try to encourage a bit of teaching on the wards and sympathetic attitudes, but just as a person can't change their older parents, you're in a very vulnerable position as a tutor.

My idea is still, today, towards more true student status for student nurses and concentration on helping them in their emotional needs and offering them more real educational opportunities as students; all right, higher salaries when they have trained; but I think the main thing to be considered is their freedom of time, and a more mature way of teaching than is still often carried on in nursing schools. They should have a variety of experiences and be attached to an individual nursing college and perhaps be sent out to different hospitals, so that when they finish their training they know what to specialize in.

I'm also still inclined to that idea of training for people who are going to become future ward sisters and nursing sisters on the district or in a health centre. For the ones who are in superior positions, I think there *should* be a concentration on education and time to be with their tutors. A more university way is better, I think, for training student nurses, than the apprenticeship way that has been practised for years.

AS: You've now gone into the mental health field from the experiences that you've had within households and your own experience of regression and breakdown; you are also working with people in the mainstream psychiatric services. How do you go about bringing together these two rather diverse groupings of people? The impression I have is that the household and the network that you're trying to establish will have a number of links with people who have health service careers.

MB: That is true. Firstly, I would like to say that the tremendous advantage of the book to me, once it was out and published, was that I had no longer any need, at any level, to hide my background. I could use my experience – including my initial experience, in an ordinary hospital; and in the chronic wards, and Dr Werner getting me out – in a positive and a good way.

I had many, many opportunities to talk about the whole thing and to meet many people who had needs of their own. You ask how I bring diverse groupings together: educationally. I'm very thankful that I *was* taught how to teach – using visual aids and things like that – and I'm fully aware that it's not all 'talk and chalk' and 'no impression without expression'. These things stay with me and I think they help me to talk to people individually and collectively when I go round giving talks.

So there was a lot of satisfaction in being able, at last, to be open about my past, and I always like to respond when I'm asked to talk somewhere. The places have been very varied: because I paint I've been to the College of Art and Design in St Albans; I've been to a number of mental hospitals and universities, at home and abroad; I often show a few paintings as well. So, through doing this and through times when other people have interviewed me and written about me, I feel that the experience has been used in a positive way, as I say. My life has assumed an unusual nature [*smiling*] because I paint and I do some writing.

Also I'm very aware of two things. First, that it's very important that people realize there is always a possibility of psychotherapy, because some people are still sometimes meeting, when they have breakdowns, with some doctors who would just prescribe medication and not give them an opportunity to know that there is another form of help called psychotherapy. So many people are still back where I was, many years ago before I got to Dr R. D. Laing.

AS: Whom you reached through James Robertson.

MB: That's right, through James Robertson. Worse than that, they don't even know what to look for and it took me some years and Mother Michael, a contemplative nun who's dead now, to keep me geared to look for a psychotherapist. One does know it depends a bit on where you live; it's easier in London than other places, and it's not always easy to find a psychotherapist to take you on, but it's pretty awful when you don't even know there is a possibility of looking for such help.

Secondly, I feel that I can share with people who are in rather extreme states of mental breakdown. I feel they are my very special friends and over the years I have lived in other households besides Archway. I feel I have been able to offer something positive, usually to an individual person who is in a state of regression.

AS: You said to me earlier that you feel that you have become for these people a kind of parental figure and that it feels all right if your contact with them is intermittent: you play a part for them at a particular time of stress and you wouldn't seek a closer involvement. Can you say a bit more about that?

MB: You're quite right. One has to remember, if the person has wanted to really regress and they need someone to help them feed and to bathe, that you're not really the real parent, however much they may feel that you're a parental figure – like I did with Joe particularly, and to some extent with Ronnie. It's very important for you, however much they may be wanting to cling, for you to be able to get *out* quickly, the same as you would have got *in* quickly. Every person that I have been so involved with has always had a therapist, a person they go to in an office and who might come to see them. So I have been more the person who helped someone to feed and bathe, and not the person that talked to them about how they felt; but perhaps I helped them to feel more deeply, as it were.

Also, through those experiences I came to realize in little ways how different people can be. For example, when I was really very down I couldn't bear anybody to touch my hair and it got like a terrible bird's nest [*laughs*] and I had to untangle it as I started to come up out of down times; but when I was caring for Roger, I realized that he just loved me to stroke his hair and in this way he was different to me.

The more I've known people in breakdown the more I've realized that of course they're going over their particular early childhood which wasn't exactly the same as mine, though they have certain needs that are very similar. They certainly don't want to talk and I wouldn't wish to bring them up out of it by talking, as you can feel terrible if you come up too quickly; but I know they will gradually come up, for air as it were, and follow their own inclination when it's the right time. I'm also very aware that coming up is not really a problem, it's going down that's more difficult and I admire the therapists very much who, when a person is for going down, are prepared to help them to break down into their depths. I think that's a very courageous and difficult thing to do, more than supportive therapy as such.

I think that I had some inkling of that, years and years ago, because I was very interested to read – I think in the nursing press – of an experiment that was carried out at the Maudsley Hospital in London. They regressed children, I think only about seven or eight years of age, to sucking bottles and other things. I don't think it's been done since, but it rather touched my insides at the time, though it was many years before I ever went down like that.

Of course I didn't know exactly how it was going to happen when I went to Kingsley Hall, though I originally had told Ronnie that I wanted to go back to before I was born and come up again. But only as I started to go into it did I slowly come to realize that it didn't just mean talking about it, I was really . . . [*hesitating*]

AS: really enacting it –

MB: . . . in a real way, yes, a baby. It was much more, in a way, than what you would call psychodrama. I don't want to belittle psychodrama because a lot of people got a lot from it – as a way of expressing a lot of emotion – but I was really *me*. I wasn't acting a baby. It sounded like a baby crying when I cried and I couldn't take a lot of things that you would normally be able to take; I would have lost myself in my words. I couldn't really afford to talk and I didn't open my eyes much when I was really down; it was too much, I didn't want to look. (If you think of it, of course, sight only comes after a baby is out of the uterus.) Smell was also very important to me. One's senses are very heightened in these states and water meant a lot to me; that's why I was very glad, ultimately, to be involved in the work of Karel Ringoet with underwater swimming and diving.

To be with someone when they are in a very low state, that's quite important; but it's also *very* important, as I say, that you get out as they start coming up and out. My contact with other

people has made me realize how powerful that role is, apart
from my own experiences of how strong the contact of Joe to
me could be. I can meet Joe quite socially now; I'm not in therapy
with him and we have a good contact, and I'm not in an awful
state because Joe has said A or not said B or something like
that . . .

AS: Or is talking to someone else anyway . . .

MB: Exactly [*laughs*], and I'm dead jealous or something like
that. What I have realized when I've had contact with other people, at least to some extent, is that I was in a very powerful
role in relation to them and I must be considerate for how they
feel. The biggest thing that could upset them was if I unnecessarily
were to be going away from them. I often stayed bodily a long
time with them, you see, *near* them. But as they came up and
out I would wish to withdraw. Mind you, when they've come
up and out, they haven't continued the dependence on me which
I continued with Joe after Kingsley Hall. I've not seen them
in an office situation, they've had somebody else to do that.

But what I *have* noticed is that they will write when something
special has happened. For example, Roger wrote to me from
the States when he got married, or when he started to work and
his wife worked also as a therapist in Philadelphia. Out of the
blue I heard recently from someone else when she moved her
address. It's usually, I notice, when they've had some quite big
change in their lives. Whether that happens or not we often
exchange Christmas cards.

AS: It seems to me that you then become an attachment figure.
You're mentioning that quite often you would stay bodily with
them; it's a reminder of John Bowlby's emphasis on physical
proximity in attachment relationships. I find that interesting
because you're talking about a situation in which the person in
breakdown might not be talking, would be regressed to a much
earlier stage of life in which their senses are heightened; their
sense of where safety is has everything to do with the immediate
environment, rather than a relationship mediated by spoken language. It strikes me that it may be no accident that it's at special

times in someone's life cycle that they then want to reaffirm the contact with you.

MB: Yes, I agree with you. I feel that if any reply is needed at those times it must be just a simple one of reassurance and good greetings and I wouldn't wish to prolong it. But naturally, I'm quite pleased to know that things are going quite well; I've never heard anything terrible about anybody that I had such a close contact with.

When I first went to Stockholm, around 1984, as I say, I gave a talk to the Autistic Children's Society and the Art Therapists' Group. A doctor was there and he asked me if I would visit a certain girl. Anyway, I met her. She was alone in an enclosed garden; I was on one side of the fence and she the other. The problem was extreme destructiveness from when she was a small child and she's had many years of confinement, she's thirty-two now. The second time I met her I was walking in the grounds with her parents, herself and the doctor. The doctor invited her to give me a hug and she replied quite distinctly, 'I think it is too soon for that.' She is a baby in some ways, she plays with her shits every morning and yet she's dressed and put out to walk around the enclosed garden. I felt that I wanted to bring her down from her awful divisions: she's terribly active, mentally, verbally; as well as physically in a bad way.

I was reading something of Bruno Bettelheim's recently; he writes about adolescent psychotics to whom he gives space. Just as with a baby who likes cuddling, so a baby also needs to be left alone. The girl herself has said to me, 'Mary, let's try, walk some distance from me.' But in the present situation I'm not in a responsible situation in that mental hospital and if I got hurt or the people that care for her [got hurt], there would be a lot of trouble.

I still visit her and although I have held her arm she has never with me, as with other people, resolved this problem of how to be with another human being without hitting them. (I'm told she has never hurt animals.)

My inclination, based initially on Kingsley Hall methods, was: if she doesn't want to get up let her lie on the bed and see what happens; rather than say you *must* do this or that at certain times; you must eat, you must dress, you must go out, you must come in. However, I'm also very aware that regression must not be unduly indulged in. Fortunately this person has dedicated helpers and therapists who now treat her with psychotherapy, and are helping her to progress in an integrated and more adult manner. Her English has become fluent, she's painting the walls of her room. An American therapist who recently saw her helped to resolve a lot of anger in her. Furthermore her parents consented to refrain from visiting her for some time. The psychotherapists involved with her have now established a psychotherapeutic household outside the hospital, which hopefully she will be able to join one day.

I want to point out, Ann, that there are limitations to what you can do in certain situations; I think that goes for any country. You feel you want to get in a much freer milieu to start with, where you can have a different way of looking at the whole thing. Different people in different situations can achieve similar, successful results; it depends on the circumstances and what is available. If you remember, David Cooper tried before Kingsley Hall to get something freer, Villa 21 [an experimental self-governing ward at Shenley Hospital in Hertfordshire], but it was realized it wasn't a very good place to do it in. I know a doctor who's trying something similar in his own part of the country, but he's having great trouble with the authorities. I would do everything I could to help, and I've gone and talked to his nurses (he's trying to train a few nurses in psychotherapy). I still feel he's got an especially difficult job trying to do it within that environment. All the same, you can do something; and I would never refuse an opportunity to go and give a talk in a psychiatric hospital. And I have done many times over.

AS: Is there any pattern of responses, when people hear you talk; are there issues that come up again and again in discussion?

MB: By and large I'm thankful to say that responses are usually quite encouraging, but one thing immediately comes to mind. I remember being on a panel once on television, about the time the book came out, and somebody from the audience did mention that they thought we were the black sheep. This was a reference to the Kingsley Hall participants, I think because of the emphasis on 'no them and no us', as Ronnie Laing says. But, by and large, I have quite a lot of positive and encouraging responses.

Mind you, the very fact that they ask me means that they want to hear or are interested to hear that angle, or they certainly wouldn't ask *me* to go and talk to them. Sometimes I show the Swedish video; Gerard's questions are very good and it gives some idea of my experience. I would be sometimes eager to point out that Kingsley Hall was an experimental place and in forming a household we do not anticipate that all people will necessarily go through a deep regression or necessarily have need to, as I did.

I also think, Ann, that in some ways I probably have a much easier time than Joe or Ronnie would, simply because some people would still tend to see me as the one who has been helped. Whereas they might tend to say quite critical things to Ronnie, they might be a bit hesitant to say them to a person that they would half see as a patient.

AS: How interesting . . .

MB: Well, I don't see myself as a patient at all. I believe in Ronnie's saying that there must be no rigid 'that's staff and that's patient'; and that if you had good help yourself there's a chance you may be of use to others. In any case you have a natural good feeling with them when they are in those states.

I fully realize I'm not magic and I try my best, if people have got any of those ideas about me and think that if I just go and talk to them something marvellous will happen; but of course as you and I know, any sort of therapy is jolly hard work, and it's skill from the therapist's side that makes for the healing process. There's no magic about it. All one can do is to try to help a person to realize that truth, but to realize also that the suffering is a suffering of growing, not absolute deadness, dead feeling.

It's a suffering that will help you to come to your own life. There's a world of difference between hiding a problem away in a cupboard and looking at a problem. I always think that electric shocks are a bit like a bang on the head or shutting somebody in a cupboard, rather than any degree of understanding, *any* degree of understanding. About tablets: well, as Joe says, 'they're an internal strait-jacket'. That does not mean to say I absolutely disagree with any medication any time, but I do think that if a medically qualified psychotherapist puts a person on medication they put them on it with the idea of taking them off it. A wholesome attitude towards using medication is a world away from people that only look upon it a bit like giving insulin to a diabetic, a purely chemical thing, which you must take for the rest of your life.

AS: Have you at any time taken up directly with people your sense that they may be responding differently to you because you're the 'patient' and Joe Berke was the 'doctor', or Laing was the 'doctor'? I'm thinking of this because you told me that you and Dr Laing sat on a panel together.

MB: Yes, yes.

AS: Which would mean there would be less opportunity for the audience to create that kind of split between the doctor and the patient, if both were sitting on a panel at the same time. I wonder what kind of experience that was?

MB [*smiling*]: It was in Paris in 1986 and Ronnie's film *Knots* had just been shown. It was during a festival of films about madness. I had made a short film [see below, pp. 76–8] but on this particular occasion my film was not shown, so Ronnie got more questions than I did. But I remember towards the end he was asked what his current research was and he said something about witches and women. Then somebody else piped up [*mock scholarly tone*], 'Oh and Mary Barnes, may we ask what is your current line of research?' At the time I'd been up in Scotland trying to get something started with a group that had disintegrated and I'd come back to the South. My things were still up in Scotland and I remember that I just immediately responded by saying

– 51 –

'Actually, my research at the moment is very practical. My paintings and some of my stuff are up in Scotland; I'm living in Scotland
and I'm trying to find somewhere to live in the South' [*laughing*].
This was the end and they just laughed; somebody thanked us
for our contributions and appearance and we all went to a restaur-
ant to eat. I have never been made to feel, of course, by Ronnie
and Joe, that I was the 'patient' and they were the 'doctor'; that's
entirely contrary to their line of thought.

AS: On the other hand, everyone lives in a world in which those
kinds of distinctions operate.

MB: Absolutely.

AS: And in your working relationship with people working in
the hospital system you are interacting with people who have
a professional identity. You need presumably to observe the con-
ventions within which they work, and if you're trying to negotiate
with hospital authorities you have to make some kind of relationship on their terms. It strikes me as a complicated issue.

MB: Right. I do my best to negotiate it the best I can. It's like
being in a river in a canoe, and you're negotiating the rocks
and you're in the current.

Well, once I was on a committee to do with good practices
in mental health and we used to sit in boardrooms of hospitals
in different places. I used to feel that they didn't quite know
what to make of me sometimes. When I went to Glasgow, for
example, I went round to visit a few medical doctors and therapists
– both working in the NHS and privately – to see what interest
there might be in the possibility of a household; whether they
would be interested in suggesting the household to some of their
clients that they might feel would have a need for such a living
environment; and would be generally helpful and part of the
network. Often I would err on the safe side; I remember during
one interview instinctively saying Dr Edith; I didn't say the full
name, but I said Dr before the christian name. On the other
hand, when I go out to Stockholm it is as it has been from the
beginning [with the doctors]: Elgard is Elgard and Nora is Nora
and we're all on a level. But of course they're very involved

1 Mary Barnes and Joe Berke, the attic, Hampstead, 1971

2 Painting *Peter the Fisherman* at Kingsley Hall, 1968

3 *Three Stages of Sacrifice: The Lamb in Fire, Christ on the Cross, Christ as the Host (Consecrated)*, 1969. This painting was originally on the dining-room wall at Kingsley Hall.

4 *Crucifixion*, wall of my room on the roof, Kingsley Hall, January 1966

5 *Foetal-like Figures*, wall of my room on the roof, Kingsley Hall, January 1966

6 *The Cross of Christ*, Kingsley Hall, December 1969

7 *Nativity*, Saint Dympna's, Seaton, Devon, 1980

with residential therapy work, which is a bit different from somebody working in a clinic. I remember that when I first met Jim [a PA doctor] down in the hospital in Exeter, I'd been talking to him for a time and I said, 'What do you feel? Can I call you Jim?' He just hugged me, so I felt he was one of us, as it were. This I always feel is helpful to me because I like to be accepted as Mary; I don't really like being labelled as anything.

Occasionally, if I would have to fill up a form I have put writer and painter; I have sometimes put just painter. By and large, I don't use my nursing qualifications; I'm SRN [State Registered Nurse], STD [Sister Tutor's Diploma]. But if I felt I was going into a particular situation with an authority and it would make a difference to the work [to use my qualifications], then I might well do so. I try to keep an open mind, I think that what you have to know is inside; and if you are putting on something you wouldn't choose all the time you must know you're just putting it on for the minute.

AS: Because it has a purpose.

MB: That's right. I was once in a room in Basel where a person named Angela had a flat. She was a young married woman who had absolutely not wanted medication, and was being helped by Professor Benedetti of Basel University in much the way that I had been by Joe and Ronnie (although it was her husband, a university man, who used to do the cooking and the shopping and household things for her). I said to Professor Benedetti, 'I'm not a therapist in the way that I see people in an office and have a practice in England.' He said, 'Oh Mary, you are more than a therapist.' So we all felt happy with that and I just considered myself Angela's friend. Maria [in Stockholm] always says that I'm her special friend – not that, actually locked up as she is, she has any opportunities in general of making friends; but I'm well satisfied to be that.

I remember what Ronnie Laing once said: he used to talk at the dinner table sometimes at Kingsley Hall, and it was very enlightening, if you would have an ear to listen to what was being said. He was once trying to convey that what really mattered

was what he called 'presence'*, it was your presence that meant
so much [rather than your label]. (So often I have met people
in household situations and you honestly wouldn't know whether
they had come to live there and had need for therapy, or whether
they were visiting therapists. Mistakes actually have been made
because people haven't known beforehand and haven't thought
out instinctive reactions: say somebody is the Medical Director
of some hospital somewhere, but you don't know that and they
come just as another person.) So I can understand exactly what
Ronnie means when he talks about presence; it's your presence
that matters.

There's so much in institutional life that, perhaps without people consciously thinking what they're doing, has taken away that
possibility: routines and uniforms, and all sorts of other things
in the past. It's extremely difficult for people when they have
tried to do away with it. It seems to be in the very walls of
the place, so that people instinctively behave in certain ways
because they are in that building. At times I've felt that, and
without having a bundle of keys (and in some places I think
the more keys they've had the more important position they were
assumed to have). That is so baffling, bewildering and so harmful
to a person who's already mentally upset anyway, before they
enter such a place.

I feel, therefore, that the true places of healing of the future
should be small groups that we call psychotherapeutic households,
as I say, and material resources and people should be concentrated
towards real depth understanding. People should be paid money
whilst they're having therapy training, encouraged to have therapy training. All this should start with student nurses and medical
students, before they really get into the swing of their professional
lives.

---

* In Joe Berke's words: 'Authority could only be established by what
Ronnie referred to as "presence". "Presence" has to do with all that
which leads other people to respect you.' (Barnes and Berke, 1971,
p. 260). [AS]

I think it is good in this country that people who especially want to have psychotherapeutic training – if it's really relevant to their make-up and their personalities, and they can be of use to other people – can have opportunities to continue without necessarily having a medical or psychology degree. I'm not saying that general nursing and medical knowledge isn't a help with somebody in breakdown states, because you do have some idea of how their bodily state is – some people get very frightened if they get a rapid pulse or other symptoms which are not in themselves dangerous. So it is, in many ways, an advantage, but it can also, initially, be a stumbling block because you've been taught so strongly certain attitudes as a trained general nurse, never mind trained mental nurse.

AS: I feel this brings us back to the issues that we were talking about earlier, when you spoke of your familiarity with Isabel Menzies' work. In a sense, it seems to me that you're saying that potentially those nursing skills could be of use, but they're being taught within social structures and nurse training systems which have inculcated defences against the terrific anxiety that proximity to physical and mental illness arouses [Menzies, 1959].

MB: Yes, absolutely.

AS: The other issue that I want to come to was raised by your speaking of your enacting your own situation when you were at Kingsley Hall. It was different from psychodrama, you said, because 'I really was me'. On the other hand, there's been drama in the form of David Edgar's play *Mary Barnes* [Edgar, 1979]. Can you tell me a little about that? I know you've just seen it staged again at a drama school in London.

MB: Yes, at the Mount View School; they were just finishing their three-year course. The person who played me played me very well, and I think that she's about the youngest person I've ever seen in the part.

The play, I think, was of great educational value to a lot of people because people wrote to me, and they wrote to the PA. I think some people may have found a psychotherapist as a result of seeing the play and consequently really seeking that sort of help. I thought it was very clever [*laughs*] of David Edgar to put into the words of the person who, if you knew the different characters – some of them were a bit jumbled up – you would have realized, at that moment anyway, was the Ronnie figure saying, 'Curing, if I may say so, is something that you do to bacon', because Ronnie sees the whole thing as a growing life process. He would never make strict lines: 'he is sick, she is well'.

I think there is no particular virtue in being what you call 'normal', in the way that normal is being like the majority. Genius isn't normal, sanctity isn't normal. I think that there are many extremes that may even be tolerated in one culture and not in another; it does go into wide and political issues. I think Joe and Ronnie have explored that much more than I have or ever would do, but I do see similarities in certain religious terms and terms used by the analysts of today.

I think depth understanding is very much in the hands of the analysts today. There was one analyst who said to me, 'It's got buried; it *was* in the Church' (meaning the Christian Church a few centuries ago). I think I would agree with that, because I've read the lives of some saints and they certainly went through some pretty queer experiences that we would have said were mad; and in terms of what was then called 'spiritual direction' they must have been got through it.

On the other hand, when you think of some things that I experienced in Kingsley Hall, rather than on my feet in a convent – because I couldn't have been kept [in a convent] and got through it, as Mother Michael realized – you understand that there are times in one's life when one can't sustain one's everyday responsibilities. But at a deeper level, I do think there are similarities between the therapeutic household and some religious practices throughout the ages. I certainly fasted, I had solitude, and I knew physical pain in the body without physical sickness. All these things various religions have been very aware of in their conscious desire for wholeness and holiness for centuries.

St John of the Cross said, 'To suffer the darkness is a way to great light.' A lot of hermits went off alone into the desert and I think they must have resolved a lot of anger in their times of solitude; Buddhist monks certainly fast and other religions do as well. The body is very involved in the ways different religions consciously go towards their wholeness.

I also think that, with regard to the soul and the level below words, one has to somehow get down there. It's something like the instinctual way of following your own light. I think that if you're in touch or back in touch with something that must have happened when you were born or before you were born, then that can be very helpful. Because even if you don't completely know exactly what you're going after or doing at the time, with that half glance back later you can see that it's no wonder A or B happened.

Some people would say that's providence and some use the word destiny; Ronnie talks about expanded consciousness; and I might say the widening of one's vision. I do think there is something very akin in us to the instinctual sort of knowledge that animals have: like a bird knows when to fly and when to migrate; and a baby knows when to be born. It's something at that level.

AS: A baby knows when to be born, but a baby also depends on a form of good-enough mothering or parental care; and these forms of care can be inadequate or, in some cases, absent.

MB: Oh yes, yes.

AS: Hence some of the difficulties that lead people into breakdown, or into psychotherapy.

MB: And away from their true . . . what's the word that I want [*hesitating*] . . . not exactly path –

AS: Centre?

MB: Centre, that's the better word; or wavelength, some people might say. They're not exactly off route, they're . . .

AS: Off course.

MB [*animated*]: Off course, that's the word. Something in them has the feeling that they want to go back in order to go forward, which is regressing: going back in order to go forward.

AS: Yes, if one does go forward, but not –

MB: If one gets stuck.

AS: Stuck.

MB: In the regression.

JULY 1988

4

PAINTING, WRITING
AND GIVING TALKS

AS: Had you done any painting before you were in Kingsley Hall?

MB: No, I hadn't. As a child, unlike my brother, I hadn't had much inclination towards it at all, yet I think there was something in me that drew me towards painting. I remember when I was doing the tutors' course at Hull University, and during a study tour in Norway, I saw some paintings on the wall of a church in the dim candlelight; I was very drawn towards these paintings. Consciously I thought it must be terrible to be a painter and not to be able to paint; but I never thought that I really had a desire myself to paint, although I was aware that my brother was considered very good at painting when he was a child and that my mother did very nice, delicate water-colours, as I say. She did tell me that she didn't think I had much ability with my hands and I think that influenced me as a child.

When I was going down into the psychotic state at Kingsley Hall and I was being encouraged to do what I wanted to do, I found black paint and painted breasts round the walls. Later, when I was up and around, Joe re-encouraged me to paint and to use oil pastels – he gave me a gift of a book and oil pastels at one point. He suggested that I paint the Crucifixion; I did many times, and the Resurrection also. Being Christian I painted in terms of that faith, obviously; I also painted trees a lot and illustrated the story that I wrote, 'The Hollow Tree' [see p. 109], for Ronnie's birthday, during the time of Kingsley Hall.

At one point in Kingsley Hall, I feared I would lose it if I didn't always use it, but I didn't necessarily feel I had to paint every day. At times when I was depressed I certainly didn't paint for periods, but I was assured that I would never lose it. That is quite true; I've never lost the conscious desire to paint. I feel I can always do it; sometimes I feel I want to do it more than others, but also I do not feel that I've got to paint every day, as it were. I can enjoy other interests and do other things, which I regard as also important in my life. But painting is certainly a very important part of it still.

AS: In a review of one of your exhibitions, I saw you described as a 'primitive'. Does the term speak to you?

MB: Yes, I think it means a very obvious, raw way of expression. Once I was referred to as an Expressionist. When the book came out, a review that's somewhere in one of my scrapbooks said that I paint very much like Van Gogh did; certainly I was always aware that I liked his work very much.

I think, above all, paintings just need to be appreciated and accepted rather than dissected and analysed. Some of the paintings of very young children and the abstract work of some mentally handicapped children I've known have been very beautiful, and sometimes recently I have felt towards doing more abstract work; but very often when I start like that, something seems to emerge from it and I end up with something I give a name to. But I don't think the label is of prime importance: it doesn't really bother me what people call it. I like just to do it and if they want to label it that's for someone else to do. I don't particularly aspire to be this type or that type of painter.

AS: So do you follow the reviews of your paintings?

MB: Oh yes, I would always read something about a painting that I'd done and exhibited. I would read it whether I agreed with it or not. But I wouldn't be concerned whether they said it was like Munch or Matisse, or Impressionist or Expressionist. This wouldn't bother me.

AS: I understand. By the same token, are there painters whom you feel influenced by or drawn to, even if your overriding concern is to express this raw sensation that you've been speaking of?

MB: I'm very moved by the French Impressionist painters, particularly. As I say, I also like Van Gogh, Matisse, Munch, Cézanne. A painting of architectural precision I may admire, but I don't feel drawn to it in the same way as I would feel drawn towards something that gives a stronger feeling. Feeling and movement seem very important to me. I could say the same about much more rigid painting – portraits, for example: I can appreciate a beautiful portrait, but again it's not something that I would tend to do very much myself. If I did it, it would be a feeling impression of the person, rather than a photographic likeness.

AS: Did you work continuously on your paintings, in a single stretch of energy, or did you return to them over a period of days or weeks?

MB: Practically always – and this still applies to my painting today – I finished a painting in the same space of time that I started it. It varies according to the size of the painting (it can take half an hour, two hours, three hours), but I practically always finish in the same space of time in which I start.

AS: You've always given the impression that your writing is inseparable from your painting. Have you worked on them both at the same time?

MB: Very often, yes. When I started to write stories such as 'The Hollow Tree' or a poem like 'Song of the Moon' then, instinctively, I painted and wrote almost simultaneously. Some other writing I have done without painting, and in some cases I have later illustrated it; but there's quite a lot that I haven't attempted to illustrate. It just depends on how I feel and whether I have the urge to put words to the painting or painting to the words. Joe once wondered whether I would like to write purely imaginative and fictitious writing; for example, a novel. I remember at the time I said, 'Oh Joe, it's not that I'm not appreciative

of literature as such; I am, but I feel for myself it must be true.'
True in the sense that I am writing about my own life, or people
and things that really happened or that I experienced.

AS: What do you think draws you again and again to religious
imagery?

MB: I think because my faith, as my madness in the past, has
been so powerful; they are such powerful influences in my life
[see also Barnes and Berke, 1971, p. 378].

AS: What about your own reading?

MB: I read very little technical, psychological writing nowadays.
In the past I would have read a lot, though the only parts that
I actually studied for a tutor's diploma were educational psychology and general psychology. I wouldn't go out of my way,
now, to read a lot of case histories or analytical psychological
books.

AS: So when you had the connection with James Robertson and
John Bowlby, you were reading psychoanalytic work.

MB: Oh yes, I would have been. I would have been looking
very much for writing about psychotherapy and schizophrenia
and anything psychotic; and you didn't find much in those days.
I had an external appreciation of my own needs which was not,
until I got to Ronnie Laing and then Kingsley Hall, really in
any way satisfied. Since then I seem to have got so much into
my own thing, my own self, that although I've been interested
in individual ways with other people's lives – those that have
made an impact upon me are usually people that I've been
involved with in a helping way – I haven't, in a more general
way, wanted to read technical literature as such. I've read all
Ronnie's books as they have come out, and I have an interest
in what he may write in the future; and certainly in Joe's writings.
I would like very much to read the Philadelphia Association papers
when you publish them, but those are more personal connections.

I think on the whole I paint more than I write nowadays, and
perhaps it's true to say that very often I read out what I've already
written more than I write new things (I always take some pieces
of my own writing, my stories, when I go to talk anywhere).

It just depends on the time and the interest, and where I am, as to how much I read. If I feel that it's wanted by the audience then I read more than I otherwise would.

AS: I was wondering what kind of preparation you do when you give talks, because I see you've given an enormous variety of talks in an enormous variety of places, both in this country and abroad. Are they all very different? Are you asked to talk about your own experiences, about your approach to mental health work, about Kingsley Hall?

MB: Firstly people from the analytical world want me most of all to talk about my own experiences. If, for example, I would be talking to art therapists – as I say, I once went to St Albans to the college which runs a course for art therapists – then I would tend to concentrate a bit more on the times I've done a lot of paintings. If I would be at a mental hospital, for example, and there were nurses there, I would tend to make some links with my own past nursing experience and would try to stress how you feel in a breakdown; how people can become parent figures, and how important the immediate people next to you are. How bathing and feeding people and helping them dress gives one in certain ways a situation of potential therapy, because it's like [being] a mother to the real child.

I went to Dartington Hall [the former progressive school in Devon] once, and there it was a more literary group. When I discussed what they would like in the discussion time, they said that they would most of all like to hear some more of my writings, so we did that. The main thing is that in giving a talk I don't like to talk too much so there is insufficient time for people to say what they may be thinking and want to say. I think it's very important that, whatever audience you have, people have adequate time to ask questions and to have some discussion.

The discussion arises from the interests of that particular audience and you cannot exactly anticipate that. A mainly artistic audience may perhaps ask questions about regression more than a more technical audience. So I try to feel my way into something with the people. Sometimes I have written a paper to read [out], if I feel it's rather an important occasion, like when I was invited to the annual symposium at a progressive Swedish hospital. But I also read 'The Hollow Tree' on that occasion, and we had a long question and answer session. I also remember writing a paper once called 'Going back to go forward and the resolution of anger and regression'.

I prefer not too vast an audience. I have had a very big one (the one in Sweden was in a cinema and the stage was high up) and I'm quite used to a microphone, but I am also used to talking to much smaller seminar groups of analytical people. Then it can be much more personal and very interesting for me, as well as for them.

AS: You're describing the way in which the material is inflected by the setting in which you talk. What kinds of impressions have you brought away from the groups that you've spoken to, of where they're at and what they're concerned with? Take, for instance, art therapy students.

MB: I would have tried to promote an understanding of painting as a creative activity, as something growing for whatever person was doing it: a tiny child, a person called mentally sick or in breakdown, a person doing it at home as a hobby, an old person taking it up much later in age. I would try to stress the importance of the painting being appreciated and accepted for what it was, rather than closely analysed. I think the importance to the individual who does it is that it is a means of their expression, and consequently of their growth, and it asks to be accepted for what it is. I well remember at St Albans, giving away a few oil pastels at the end. During the talk I had said that in my own therapy my work had never been analysed by my therapist – at least not to me, directly – in the way of, 'Why did you do this, Mary, why did you do the other?' We had never talked about it at that level. I remember in the morning session a professor who had worked a lot with children under the Notre Dame nuns in Scotland had spoken about saying to the nuns and the children, with regards to their artwork, 'Listen if the child spontaneously says why they do this or that in the painting, but don't seek to make suggestions or question it, just accept it.'

I said the same thing, but I don't think this was the way the students had been taught. Despite what had been said, at the end of the day the professor and his wife and myself were hurrying off to get a car to get to the station, and these students to whom I had given some oil pastels were literally running after me saying 'Oh Mary, tell us please, why did you do this and why did you do the other?', wanting reasons. So I think there are different levels of approach, and although Joe and Ronnie appreciated my painting and would certainly not dismiss it or not look at something, they certainly didn't attempt to give me an analytical interpretation of it.

AS: By analytical you mean psychoanalytical . . .

MB: Exactly, not the artistic term. If the person wants to tell you why they did this or that, all right; but if they don't it can be helpful to *you*. You can see at once: 'No wonder the person has done this figure so beautifully, now they are together; they were doing all these messy bits before. It's because of their inner state. What they've done at time B they could not have produced at time A and vice versa.' Painting does show, of course, the inner state, but I don't think it's necessary, unless the person wants to suggest something themselves, to delve into it in that way. I think the therapeutic value is in putting pen or finger to paper or doing something with clay. It's of great help to the person themselves.

A lot of very powerful painting is not something that in a superficial way you would say was beautiful. Sometimes in a state of breakdown, as with me, people paint in a very powerful manner. Why certain people like certain paintings, I think, is because something in the painting touches them deep inside; you can never tell, with a variety of paintings, which person will like what painting. That's why I always like to show a certain number of paintings to a person if I want to give them one and I happen to hear them say 'Oh, I do like that.' And you think, well thank goodness I didn't give them the other.

You can't really tell, as regards what people like. It's a very personal thing, apart from the wider thing of fashion and fame; people will buy something because sometimes maybe they think the person might become famous and they'll sell it for a lot of money afterwards. That's another reason; but that's not a reason of such great interest to the painter. You have to be true to yourself with all art. You paint in the way that it is within you to paint; that is the main point. If you try to be exactly as another painter was, that's not really you being you. I think the same applies to writing, of course, as well.

AS: A few years ago – leaving aside art from the moment – you went to talk to the Oxford Psychoanalytical Forum and the Cambridge Psychoanalytic Society.* Those must have been different settings again.

MB: Yes, in Oxford I was in the School of Experimental Psychology. I've done talks twice there, with a very big audience the first time and the second time with a smaller one. The second time I showed paintings, and it was more personal. When it was the bigger audience there were lots of questions about anger.

AS: How interesting. I remember that running through the whole of the book is the problem of 'it', anger. The Oxford audience picked that up very rapidly.

MB: Yes. Experimental Psychology arranged the meeting but it was open, so there were graduates and undergraduates. They didn't have an awful lot of opportunity to study analytical work, and it was rather behaviourist – we seemed to be rather at cross-purposes.

I also went up to the Littlemore Hospital, one of the more progressive hospitals, and there it was rather a small group including some nurses, social workers and doctors, a mixed audience.†

* Talk in the public series 'Personal Views and Ventures on Schizophrenia', Oxford, November 1983; Seminar, 'Breakdown: Going Back to Go Forward', Oxford, May 1985; Seminar, 'Disintegration, Regression and Renewal', Cambridge, October 1985.

† Seminar, 'The Experience of Disintegration', Marlborough Unit 'Seminars on Schizophrenia', May 1985.

Again, because I was asked to bring some paintings I showed some paintings, but the discussion was, you would say, on a more personal level; though somebody did mention some of the patients they had had contact with in the hospital.

They do that sometimes if you're talking to a professional group. They would ask me what I would think of somebody; or maybe they would take me to see some people. Then I would just talk as a friend to whoever I met amongst the residents in a hospital. Some of the people at the Littlemore were visitors, I remember. In a village quite near Oxford a priest and his wife (who is a therapist) are carrying on the work of Frank Lake with regards to arranging clinical theology seminars and the further publication of Frank Lake's works. They were invited to Littlemore at the same time and, if I recall rightly, something was said about primal therapy and the work of Frank Lake.

So it does vary very much. Obviously the first time I went to Stockholm I didn't know the people who were asking the questions, but, as I say, the person who turned out to be Maria's father asked a lot about aggression: how we dealt with it in the PA households and in the Arbours. One often feels probably there is a personal element in the question, but I wouldn't say anything publicly out of respect for the person's wishes with regards to that.

AS: Do you ever find it tiring going to talk to groups?

MB: I find it very stimulating, and in that way it's helpful to me. Sometimes when I have been new in a place, like first in Devon, where I didn't meet people involved in therapy work for some time, I have felt in some difficulty with regard to the amount that I could express. The difficulty on their side is partly of knowing what to ask. If it is a group, you have to know a certain amount to ask a question.

If you are a long period with other people in general, as I was in the early days in Devon, without talking of things that really matter to you, it is a bit like being faced by a wall or a rock that you feel you want to soften. So you often have to contain yourself rather than express yourself and that can be quite difficult at times.

It's the same thing as in a household. You feel very loving towards some people, but because they're in such a state they cannot accept love. You again contain something in yourself you would have preferred to express. If there is an inability – however unconscious, it's not necessarily a conscious desire or fault on the part of the other people – it's because of their past backgrounds and experience that certain things can't be accepted. Then you must retain these things until it's a good moment to express them. This is something I've tried to convey when I've been asked to speak to groups.

AS: You've been saying that when you give talks, people frequently express great interest in how anger or aggression were dealt with in PA households. Let's bite the bullet and look at that one. Not just the anger one might have felt within oneself; but anger that one might have elicited in others.

MB: Well, to speak of my experience in Kingsley Hall with regards to anger; personally, I feel I resolved quite a lot when I was lying alone in my room. I would have expressed it then as 'sweating it out' as opposed to being helped to give Joe or Ronnie a bash, or to some degree painting it out. Other people could upset me to the point when I would want to hit them; fortunately I never actually hurt anyone, and I was never actually hurt physically. But, for example, there was one youth who I think I felt very much as my brother. I would romp with him, but when he was really getting angry and, as I put it, 'seeing red', then I would whisper to him to please get off me, leave me alone. He never actually hurt me, but once he was running around with a hammer and one of the therapists came up to me – I was instinctively going to grab it – and stopped me, and said, 'Ssh, don't shout, Mary.' I didn't shout and I got to know that if a person is towards getting in a panic with anger, you can make it worse if you shout at them. You are more likely to invite them to hit you than if you speak quietly.

I remember one man who was very angry and was tearing

around the place at one time – I felt very towards him [sic];
he was a very kindly person, really. He suddenly said at dinner
one evening, looking across the table at me [*emphatic voice*],
'And *she's* the only one who understands me'. I felt quite frightened, because I was not really very grown at the time; quite
regressed. But I think something in me touched something in
him and I remember I was not afraid when he was bashing around
the place. I simply said to him, 'Just leave those things alone'
– I had some little clay sculptures – and he didn't touch them.
In a certain way – like a child feels friends with its brothers
and sisters – I had a sort of inner feeling towards people who
were behaving at times very much as they felt, and those people
were very often very frightened underneath.

I had high regard, for example, for Jeremy [a resident]. Once
somebody came to my room one evening – she was someone
well-known to the household, a friend of somebody who lived
in the house – and said would I come downstairs to speak to
Jeremy. There was a new man in the house; he had just come
as a resident, and was obviously a very fragile and frightened
person. Jeremy had hold of him on the stairs. Jeremy himself
was in a rather psychotic state and was saying, 'Throw him out,
throw him out'. I remember I trapped Jeremy and I said, 'No
Jeremy you don't throw out'. I got hold of the man and I said
to him, 'Where is your room?' He took me downstairs to his
room. I think I must have been a bit babylike, but I sat him
on the bed and said, 'Now tell me, who is your therapist?' Afterwards I left him in the room alone and Jeremy left him alone.

Later I realized the underneath whys and wherefores of that.
Jeremy had had five or six younger brothers, and it was a real
trial for him when a new person, a man, came into the house.
I think Jeremy must have felt that he missed out a lot when
he had so many younger brothers and didn't get the attention
that perhaps he had when he was a very tiny baby. He was
threatened, in other words.

AS: What you're describing sounds like a culture in which the
verbal expression of aggression was permitted but not its physical

acting out. There was a boundary to what couldn't be tolerated in the house.

MB: Exactly, one must not actually physically hurt another person. But of course, as you can imagine, tempers did run high and, thank God, nobody actually was hurt by another person. When my paintings were down I remember I got hold of a woman then as if I was going to hit her; but I was also very frightened myself and I don't think I would have really hurt her. Somebody got hold of me and said, 'leave her' and I left her.

But at times, when I felt very afraid of my aggression I *would* be able to hit one of the men who I understood was a therapist; I would never have done it to another person who I did not see as a therapist. For example, once I was obviously feeling very angry sitting in the bed and Paul [Zeal] was bringing me some food. Paul must have felt that I was near bursting point and there was a need for me to get it out. So he complained to me as if I was a mother figure; I think it was about his back or something physically wrong with his body. That really made me burst; it broke the bubble and I threw the plate on the floor. I was very angry and then Paul went out of the room and I was very terrified of being nearly killed for doing this dreadful act, but he came back with another plate of dinner and all was well.

There were other times at Kingsley Hall when I couldn't express anger directly, although I was literally stuck in my body with IT. Ronnie, at exactly the right moment, brought it out of me by making an intentionally sharp remark [see Barnes and Berke, 1971, p. 177]. He knew that it was freezing my body, but that it had to be brought out and I was terrified to lay alone inside my room. Well, after that Joe put me to bed, gave me some milk and that was the beginning of my second time down. I was able to lay with my fear of laying with it alone in the room, you see.

AS: You're saying that Ronnie bringing the anger out enabled you to go further down.

MB: Oh, yes, the second time. That was a particular incident that was purposely done to help me at a particular moment.

AS: I see you're not talking about the process of containment within, for example, analytic psychotherapy – the verbal intervention which can 'hold' an experience within the person, to make it less toxic. This is the use of words to enable someone to go into an experience which is still more broken down.

MB [*animated*]: Exactly. Yes, exactly. And this, I think, is a very great skill and a matter, of course, of timing. Ronnie Laing is very good at that: he doesn't just know what to do and how to do it, but *when*.

Thinking of the house as a whole, I would find it much more difficult to convey to you the interbalance of the feelings within a particular group. Now Ronnie and Joe were very aware of this: I remember Ronnie saying at the dinner table once, 'where's so and so, go and get somebody'. It was to do with the emotional balance of those people in that particular group. I can remember the person didn't want to come down and of course no force was applied – they were left in the room, you didn't have to come to dinner – but I can remember Ronnie rather wanting that particular person at the table at that moment.

That was something that I couldn't be so aware of, being so involved in myself; as therapist figures, Joe and Ronnie were very aware of the whole group situation in that house. Yet, looking back, I realize I was an influence, even if nobody saw me for weeks – when I was in my room and only Noel and Paul were bringing me food or Joe was coming in the door (in the beginning the door was always open but people weren't coming in, and then later on I had the door shut). As I say, I do appreciate I was an influence in that house, but not in a way that was at all obvious to many people.

AS: I'm wondering about differences between therapy practised in a household setting and in a consulting room; I'm thinking, for example, of a paper by Haya Oakley in Free Association Books' collection of Philadelphia Association papers [Oakley, H. 1989]. She describes doing psychotherapy with a resident in a PA household and some of the difficulties that are presented when she goes to a social gathering at the household. Her patient/client

wants to keep her all to himself and she has to say 'no', she has to create a boundary. At Kingsley Hall, boundaries were not set around conventional roles, but around what could be borne psychically. Where do you feel you are at on some of these issues?
MB: Kingsley Hall was a very raw experience for the therapists, as well as for all the other people there. The barriers were so down. When Joe hit me for example, he got a lot of guilt about it, and yet it was something that nobody in the house, I think, would have in any way criticized him for doing. On the contrary, it was a time when I was very unpopular and probably people thought, 'she sure asked for it'. There was nothing objectively wrong in it, so far as I see, though it's not the sort of thing that would have got by in a conventional setting of a hospital, or in conventional psychotherapy. But then there are many things, good things, that can happen in such a milieu that can't happen in a hospital.

Kingsley Hall was more true to an ordinary way of living. An ordinary child sees their parents at their worst, they see them at their best; and as they get older I think they have great love for their parents, as I say. Far from being critical, they appreciate the difficulties of the parents' situation; and I think that as one comes through a situation like Kingsley Hall one completely understands how with my release of anxiety I looked much younger, and Ronnie Laing tended to look much older by the end of it. One realizes all the burden of his anxieties and what he was holding. It's a very tricky situation, especially with a group, to hold or contain the anger and yet to let it go; and this is precisely what was being done at Kingsley Hall.

It had to be held in every sense of the word, not just in the house but in the road outside and with the official authorities. Certain things could easily have put a full stop to the work many times over before the end of that five years. All this was very anxiety-provoking to Ronnie, and I'm quite certain I wasn't very helpful in easing that in any way at times; although the only time I was actually aware of trouble personally with neighbours was when they complained because I was screaming and crying a lot in very early days. But I didn't have personal difficulties with the road outside because when I was running along the road people accepted me as the child I was. The hardware store man gave me sweets; when I was going shopping with Joe, we were accepted; but other people tended to have more difficulties and the house as a whole wasn't easily accepted. The play brings that out very well, very well.

Nowadays I would be inclined to merge into a locality with a household, if the decision were left to me. In the beginning with Kingsley Hall they made attempts to communicate with the local people, not only with the people who were living in the house at the time and who gradually left, but with the local residents – and in that particular locality people were particularly liable to not understand anything at all about what was afoot and not to be sympathetic. Of course you have to discuss the matter with the local DHSS, as regards finance for the people coming to the house. But the more a house can be quietly there, and just be accepted as part of the locality, the more, I think, it's better than going too much out of your way to explain. I remember Ronnie once said, 'never complain, never explain', and I think I know exactly what he meant.

At Kingsley Hall, there was a tremendous respect for people without any labels attached, as I say, and you really couldn't always tell whether a visitor was a therapist or somebody coming to live in the house: sometimes they were very covered, and didn't take the lid off until they came to Kingsley Hall, and they could appear very intellectual. There could be little groups sitting in the kitchen talking what I would have said was big psychological talk, you know, and using lots of technical terms. Well, of course, it was not good for them because it was stopping themselves from going into their own depths by talking about it. Needless to say I didn't get involved with such groups.

But I'm aware that if you have functioned professionally as a therapist it could be difficult just to let yourself be, because if you're going to go down emotionally as I did – and many others did to some degree – then if you're turning it over in your mind or trying to look at yourself or be analytical with your own state of being, then it might stop you from going down. My difficulty, in later times when I got very anxious, was to stop talking. In the very beginning I would have had difficulty in expressing inner feelings to a therapist but, during Kingsley Hall times and after, there have been times when I've wanted to withdraw and I've had great difficulty in shutting up [*laughs*].

AS: Let's say something more about the play. It brought the Kingsley Hall period into a much wider focus and I think gave it a whole new generation of audiences. When I looked at the review of the play in your scrapbooks, I was reminded of its enormous success. Yet it seems to me that there's something of a paradox in the reception of the play. In order for the play to have the immediate resonance that it has had, in so many places and countries, there has to be something about your experience that touches other people; on the other hand, we know that not everyone is in breakdown or becomes psychotic. Winnicott's suggestion that the *fear* of breakdown is one of a group of universal phenomena [Winnicott, 1974], so enabling an empathetic response, strikes me as relevant to this.

MB: I think what you're saying is quite true. Certain points of it hit certain points in people's experience, although the whole experience is not common to the whole number of people that see the play. Certain aspects of it – perhaps not that which they're fully, consciously aware of – touch something in them and they feel a bond with people in the play, particularly with me. I think seeing the play is inevitably a very moving experience and one which is almost, I would say, compulsive looking and listening. I don't think many people would walk out of it, however much it might disturb some people that saw it.

There was a lot in the press about it and I was very thankful that the people that played in it did quite well out of it.

AS: How did the play come to be written?

MB: I think David Edgar must have asked me first about it. He wanted to come to the Archway household and make tapes with me, so I did a lot of tapes with him; a bit, Ann, as we're doing now. Later [the actress] Patti Love came down to Devon and we finger painted together. I certainly knew her better, before the play happened, than I've known anybody else who played me; other times I've seen it played but I haven't been backstage beforehand like I did at the Royal Court [Theatre in London] and had quite a close relationship with the person who was playing me.

For the actors the emotional strain was very great. When it was a matinée Patti Love had to have her throat sprayed before the evening performance, because of the screaming. She played the part from the guts up, and I think she played superbly well. Patti, I remember, said to me before the first night at the Royal Court, 'Mary, I don't want to see you in the theatre' – I think she felt it might put her off. (I sat far back in the stalls.) All the Arbours and the Philadelphia Association people were there and a lot of other people that I knew.

Simon Callow played Joe. Joe said if he had realized how good Simon would be playing him he would have had his own name, because, as you know, Simon played him as Eddie and I was the only one that actually had my own name. David Gant, who played my brother, was marvellous. David was by nature a very quiet and reserved man. He and Patti both met Peter, and David walked as Peter did and he spoke as he did. Recently, as I say, I saw the Mount View Drama School in Crouch Hill do the play; I think it's a bit easier for a person who is a bit nearer their real childhood, in some ways, to play it, because they're more able to get down into something. Eileen Atkins told me she thought she played me too intellectually when the play was at Long Wharf, New Haven around 1979; I remember I said, 'You can only play it as you can.' I've seen it played in Germany, with Jutta Eckhardt playing me; they did a very good set there. They came over to look at Kingsley Hall and it was almost exactly like the real place.

I have been very appreciative of all that David Edgar put into that play. The play was very good for me, and I think for David, and for many more people than I'll ever see in this life, but whether we'll ever get a film or not is another thing. At the time, Simon Callow said it was crying out for celluloid and it is a shame we didn't go on to a film at the time of the Royal Court.

AS: Moving up to the present day, what is your contact now with people who were so important to you at that time? How many of the original group at Kingsley Hall are you still in contact with?

MB: Very few, actually. Emma [a resident]: I'm still in contact with her and she's living in London and at the moment expecting a baby. Jeremy: I last saw him some years ago where he lives; I think he's still living in a basement flat, not so far from where the Archway household was.

AS: What about some of the therapists there, like Dr Laing for instance?

MB: The last time I saw him was at the festival of films about madness in Paris in 1986. As I say, I had made a short film the year before, with the French actress Delphine Seyrig, which was based on my painting, and a film of Ronnie Laing's *Knots* was shown at the British Council. Ronnie was there to answer questions and so was I. The festival of films was organized by Abraham Segal, who also produced this film of Delphine and me; he makes documentary films and is quite prominent in a patients' organization in Paris. (I'm not actually involved in it, I just know the people personally as I know the patients' organization in Stockholm. We in the British Isles haven't got exactly the equivalent of that, but they do help a lot of people.)

AS: What kind of people attended the festival?

MB: First, I would say, a lot of students, except for the British Council's showing of the film of *Knots*, which was by invitation only. At every other showing of any of these films you could hardly get in the door, there was hardly breathing space. It was absolutely crowded and I never really knew exactly who the majority of the people were. One would imagine the general public, as it was widely advertised.

It was Abraham Segal who brought me and Delphine Seyrig together. She was drawn to me because I had gone back a long way and because she had played madness when she had played the part of Aloïse, a painter born in the nineteenth century, who died in a mental hospital. Aloïse had, therefore, a very different experience to all that had happened in my life. Although she didn't ever get out of the hospital, her work was to some extent acknowledged and Delphine has a scrapbook full of reproductions of her painting.

The film shows me looking at this book with Delphine, and Delphine asking me some questions about my experience. Then I did a finger painting and the director filmed me doing the painting. The film was made in a very big sitting-room in the apartment of Delphine Seyrig and they had put up a big easel because it was better for the camera to show me working at an easel. I remember Delphine said to me, 'How do you usually paint?' I said, 'Oh, [for] a big painting like this I would have the canvas on the floor and I would be bent over it.' So she said to the film director, 'Take that easel away! Mary paints on the floor.' So that is how I painted it.

AS: Did you feel distant from Aloïse's experience itself?

MB: Yes I did. I felt sympathetic towards Aloïse because she could not have had really psychotherapeutic understanding. I felt perhaps that if she had been better understood she need not have spent all the rest of her life painting in a hospital.

AS: What were her paintings like?

MB: Well, to me they seemed rather tight. A lot of them were figures of women in the traditional dress of the time. They were not the sort of painting, quite honestly, that I would have wanted to possess. Again, I felt that if she hadn't been in that situation, but had been painting in a different environment, she would have painted much more freely.

AS: Do you know why she was admitted to a mental hospital?

MB: Delphine could give you an accurate and historically detailed account about it all, which I cannot, but so far as I remember she got very isolated and lonely in her adult life and went into a psychotic state. I would say she just languished in hospital, partly because there wasn't enough call from the outside to try to get her more suitable living conditions. Also one has to remember the generation she was living in: it was quite unusual to get out of hospital if you had gone into one in a psychotic state.

AS: You said that you last saw Dr Laing in Paris; you also heard him on the radio.*

MB: Yes, with Anthony Clare [1985]. Yes; I admire Clare, he's got a mind like a needle. At the time I was in Scotland with friends, having spent the day at a non-residential therapy unit, the Salisbury Centre in Edinburgh, where people do a lot of artwork and sculpture. I thought the interview was very good; I thought Ronnie was marvellous to be so open in replying to the questions, but as I say, he never makes barriers between himself and people who might have been his patients, or people like Anthony Clare who was interviewing him. He was very honest about everything, I thought.

AS: Did it disturb you to hear him talk so openly about his own difficulties, and his sense that he was in the grip of alcoholism and also a cyclical depression which he associated with his father's and his grandfather's experience before him? Did it cause you pain that he was now . . .

MB: Suffering so much?

AS: Suffering so much.

MB: No, Ann. I felt very drawn towards him and very compassionate towards his difficulties. I felt for Ronnie because he's had so many anxieties that I've never ever been near: with real children and marriages, as well as the tremendous strain of his own analytical practice and, I imagine, envies and jealousies from

---

* Interviewed in Anthony Clare's series, *In the Psychiatrist's Chair*, BBC Radio, 14 July 1985. Clare probed Laing about his own family experience, and Laing spoke openly of a depression which had beset him for the previous ten years. [*AS*]

colleagues of what he managed to do. They may not have wanted to do it, but all the same if somebody has actually done it, it doesn't mean to say that they're not envious and jealous of it. I think that Ronnie has had a terribly tough time, and I feel today that no matter what Ronnie has said or done in certain circles, he's still absolutely brilliant. In an individual therapy relationship he'll see things in a person – he reads souls, literally – that somebody else might take ages to see, if ever.

Your only feeling is that you would long to do anything you could to help. One thing I feel I can do to help is to acknowledge my tremendous debt to Ronnie; Joe also acknowledges that because he came over here [from the United States] through Ronnie. In the future ages ahead of our generation, people will look back towards Laing, at his obvious skill with psychotherapy with psychotic people. I think that much of the other criticism will fall back into the background.

AS: 'Much of the other criticism' . . .?

MB: Other people have found it very difficult to work with him. Whereas my sympathy naturally stays with him, and I appreciate all his own personal difficulties, I still feel very sad when I feel that he is being destructive to his own work and ideals.

Also his time in the PA was probably naturally almost over. So far as I can understand – and I'm on the outside more than inside – the PA needed a time to consolidate and promote further households and keep their heads above water and expand.

To a certain extent the same can be said at the Arbours, although my own feeling is that probably the most acute work is going on at Joe's crisis centre, where he has three resident therapists. But that's not to say anything against the good work of the PA. I think a lot of people are gaining knowledge and respect of the PA, and that they are probably better able to do that with Ronnie going his own way in whatever he's doing over in the States. I feel that his vital time was when he started the PA and got them on their feet. He was the burning light that led the way into the forest, as it were, and now the light has gone off on its own track.

As regards Ronnie's personal life, I think he must know that [such a form of depression] doesn't follow automatically because he's about the same age as when his father was dying in a mental hospital, and before that when his grandfather was sick. I think he must realize that it's not inevitable that he becomes like that. On the other hand, as with all families, he is probably particularly aware of it – or was at the time of that interview – because he was then the same age as when his father broke down for the second time and didn't get through it.

AS: We're nearly at the end of our time today. When you look back on your life, have you made your peace with things? You've experienced an unusual degree of suffering.

MB: Oh, yes. I feel that I've become more aware of how I can better use my free will, but also more aware of the things that we don't choose in life, for example the parents to whom we are born. So the complexity of this life is not just within ourselves, it's in the world as well. But I believe there's a Chinese proverb: 'If you want to change the world, you start with yourself.' I think that's very important. Goodness happens when it happens first within yourself.

But I am also very thrilled with exploration, in whatever way. Fortunately I was near a television set at the time, and I did see the man walking on the moon. I felt I was more used to inner exploration – the big question of the resolution of anger without the physical violence of wars. It's of *tremendous* importance to us. But I was also very thrilled with the exploration of outer space.

AS: Let's leave it there.

JULY 1988

5

'SOMETHING SACRED'
religion and psychotherapy

AS: This is our last conversation. I thought it might be good to use it to try to draw together some of the different themes that we've thought about as we've talked. I'll begin by quoting the very last sentence from your book, in which you describe the kind of place that you would like to see created in the future – 'Something sacred, full of love.' I'm using that phrase – 'something sacred' – to focus on the theme of the relationship, as you see it or as one might think about it, between states of breakdown – states of psychosis – and states of religious devotion. I've been aware, as we've talked over the last months, that much of your language is a language that derives from the Christian tradition, which is so much a part of you. You've talked about periods of fasting and periods of 'good withdrawal'; you've talked about the contrariness of Christ; about a contemplative nun who helped you greatly in the period before Kingsley Hall. You've come out with the idea that there's a similarity between religious terms of expression, and the terms used by the analysts of today.

I'm wondering how you see the realm of faith and the realm of mental health, if I can put it in that shorthand way.

MB: I feel that religious faith, in terms of any religion, is a means to an end; the end being the ultimate source of creation – God. To honestly practise a religious faith, I feel, there is a need to be emotionally free, as well as intellectually informed.

AS: At the same time, you've always spoken about your emotional difficulties in relation to family experience, haven't you, and you've talked about the space that psychotherapy offers for the individual to go over their early childhood experience. I'm wondering how you see the origin of the kind of *deep* anger that you felt you needed to get through in order to come up into what you sometimes talk about as wholeness and sometimes as holiness.

MB: I do think that beyond the bearing in the uterus, and especially the very early upbringing of the child by the parents, the emotional life of the grandparents, and beyond them of the great-grand-parents (I'm not talking about genetic inheritance here) is in some way a sort of emotional backlog that can have an influence, even several generations ahead. So you are what you are, beyond the time you were in the particular uterus through which you came into the world.

As I say, I do think that this first thing of our non-choosing – of our parents – is a part of our destiny, and that ultimately through full use of our free will (and the will isn't very free with an emotionally tangled-up person) we can not only make the best of what would seem to be a bad job, but become better as a result of the bad job. Put it like this: a person can be born with a physical disability, and yet with good development at the emotional level, and with good intention in the will can use their disability to reach quite a high degree of what – to put it in a simple way – God intended them to be.

I do think that there is a certain potential in every life, that there is a certain spirit of the divine in every living human being. The living of a life is somehow the intermingling of destiny and as full an expression of free will as possible.

AS: When you felt at your most mad – and mad is a word that you use to describe yourself; for example at the end of the book you write, 'My faith and my madness are the two great inseparable influences of my life. My madness uncovered more clearly and revealed the faith within me' [Barnes and Berke, 1971, p. 378] – did you have crises of faith?

MB [*hesitates*]: No ... no, no, no. But I certainly didn't want to get up and go running out to the church, because I felt I was in some way nearer the kernel of my being, nearer to God, than I had necessarily been at times when I was on my feet and going to church. Because I was in such a true state within myself, though it may have seemed very babylike compared to a more superficial, adult way of going on. I can remember times when I was not going out of my room and I was sat on my chamber pot – I remember distinctly reading the Mass at dawn one Christmas; I had my missal with me.

Now often when I felt very bad I didn't attempt in any way to pray in words, but I felt in a state of being where depression or darkness of the soul – as it might be said in spiritual terms – lifted a bit, and I gained a tremendous amount, I felt, with regard to my conscious acknowledgement and understanding of the faith that was in me – which I regard as something not quite of this world. You see, I think when you baptize a child, the child is receiving something that is not of this world. I know that in saying this I am speaking as a Catholic. However much you may intellectually come to disagree with it – in Catholic terms you may then be said to be a lapsed Catholic – you cannot absolutely reject the sacrament. It is something not of this world. And even though intellectually you may not give assent to it, I think there is a certain grace far below words that was given unto you through a sacrament. You have received something that nothing of this world gave and nothing of this world can take away.

I am also very aware that what is called sin and not-sin is according to the intention of the will, and what the person actually does. Feelings, in themselves, can never be sinful. One has to fully feel the anger that is within, or the sexual desire, or what have you, because those things shouldn't come to repression. But if you feel a lot of anger or hate, you don't necessarily go out and kill the person or bash someone; you can resolve it. This is akin to what contemplatives do a lot, and what the desert fathers must have done. They were alone; and I always think, of such a life, especially in the early Church, that they might not have seen external results; but their life was rather like an oil in the world. Today, no matter whether it's a question of a Christian monk or a Buddhist monk, if they individually reach a certain state of holiness that is a goodness within the world, the results of which are far beyond anything we could see in this life.

AS: When you talk about darkness of the soul, or depression, I think about our speaking also about your own destructiveness, in relation to the Kingsley Hall experience [see above, pp. 4–5]. I'm wondering if you could amplify what you mean by destructiveness – you might be thinking of hostile thoughts, anger at particular individuals, at the things that they've done, hostile fantasies about what you think someone might be thinking . . .

MB: With regard to passing thoughts, and imaginings, things that go through your mind: unless you consciously dwell upon hating another person, it can't really [*laughs*], in technical Christian terms, be sinful. As to the feeling in itself – and just as we are not in direct control of our dreams, we're not in direct control of what might pass through our minds – the point is letting it pass through rather than harbouring evil intentions in the mind.

AS: Is that how you would see the similarity between religious terms and the terms used by analysts today – the 'not-harbouring'?

MB: Yes . . . I think analysts today would encourage the person to acknowledge that which comes through the mind or is in the mind, and in many cases to express it; but not to destroy themselves or other people in the doing of it. In terms of destructiveness, I would say that although in the infant it's confined to crying and crying and hitting and hitting – it's all bodily expression – with the adult it can be in the mind and can be very harmful. I'm thinking now of malicious gossip – damaging another person's reputation; or saying *hard* things. I remember at Kingsley Hall I used to feel it was so important to keep a supple soul, a supple heart, because if the anger went hard in on you, there could be real trouble. And in some ways, at that level I think, the anger can be more damaging – even if it's not verbally expressed – than physically bashing someone.

AS: And that would be because, imperceptibly, the person towards whom you're feeling angry is going to pick up those vibes anyway.

MB: Yes indeed, yes indeed. I think this must be of extreme importance with regard to enclosed religious orders. If your mind and body are not engaged in general activities in the world at large, and you're with a few people in a comparatively small space, things are much more likely to be exposed for what they are. You're much more raw.

The whole idea of the enclosed religious order, in theory, is that the situation should be a means of purification, a means of attaining the wholeness or the holiness that you seek in this life. Therefore, to me it seems very very sad that if people who have consciously made a decision to follow what is called religious life, an openly dedicated life, should get into emotional difficulties (or the emotional difficulties surface because of the nature of the life – there's no harm in that; on the contrary), they should only end up before a medical doctor who gives them tranquillizers. This is what could happen, if there's not enough understanding of the importance of being understood as well as understanding.

AS: The Mother Superior in an enclosed religious community performs the function that psychoanalytically one might describe as holding or containing?

MB: Yes . . . yes . . .

AS: Would it be to the Mother Superior that a nun in distress – for instance, with this unresolved anger that you're talking about – would ideally go?

MB: Well, yes. She may well be confronted by the Mother Superior, or by the novice mistress, if she were not yet a professed nun, with her difficulties. For instance, she could be projecting on to the Mother Superior or the novice mistress the feelings she would have had towards her real mother. At the same time the Mother Superior herself needs to know that someone in her situation will get these projections at some time. (God alone

knows to what extent either of them would fully understand what
it was all about.) The nun would then accept help if it was available. Very often it is not as available as it might be.

I remember going to Norway soon after my book was translated
into Norwegian and talking to a Catholic psychology writer. She
said, 'I gave your book to a novice mistress in this particular
contemplative convent. There was someone there who was having
a lot of trouble, and it helped the novice mistress to sufficiently
understand the difficulties and the vocation was saved.' In other
words, the person didn't want to leave the convent; she wanted
to stay there, but something had to be sorted out and she had
to have enough understanding of whatever the particular trouble
was so she could pursue a vocation that she really wanted. In
my case I was only a postulant in the Carmel I went to, and
I hadn't any insight at all. No amount of talking in words about
my troubles could, I think, have changed my inner being. I found
it difficult that I did not have a vocation for that way of life;
it can be a very difficult situation when the person feels that
their place is in a certain convent or monastery and the majority
of the other people there don't feel that it is. And it is difficult
for the person to accept that.

Ultimately, after Kingsley Hall, I think I was seeking an assur-
ance, which I got from Mother Michael, that my vocation lay,
as she put it, in the work of Dr Laing in some way – within
the households, in trying to help spread in some way the knowledge of psychotherapy. She was very understanding, of course,
because she herself had had analytical help. Mother Michael
once said to me, 'Oh, Mary, it's all in the Bible' – but not
many religious superiors have had the advantage of depth understanding.

Depth understanding is a comparatively new understanding in
terms of the age of Christian traditions in the Catholic Church,
and some are very hesitant to use it. I remember an Irish professor,
from Dublin – this was before my time at Kingsley Hall, when
I happened to be at a conference – who once sent a nun to a
non-Catholic analyst, although there was a Catholic one, because

he considered the non-Catholic was more expert in what was required in that case.

AS: Let's talk about the differences, then, between religious practice and psychotherapy. The examples that you've given – the inner resolution of anger that was possible for the desert fathers, for example, or for those who've had a lot of solitude – are examples of parallels between these two areas of practice. But it's clear from everything you say, from the book, and from our conversations, that you believe that psychotherapy also offers something very different, if not unique. Different, not in a general sense from other forms of healing or intervention, but different from what's possible in religious terms. I wonder if you could say something about how you would characterize that.

MB [animated]: Exactly. You see, usually, religious life is very very organized, the community lives as a whole, they say the same part of the office every day, they say it together. So if a person is emotionally very immature, and goes into these strict routines, their difficulties may get very covered up.

AS: You're saying that the strict routine of a religious community can function as a defence.

MB: Oh, indeed it could. You could wear a habit – by the grace of God it didn't happen to me, I was too messed up [*laughs*] – you could wear a habit and be rather a mess underneath, and not the holy person that you might think you were getting towards being. I don't think anybody can really make it without some advice; the desert fathers had spiritual direction. If too much emphasis is put on the daily routine at the expense of something deeper, then everything could appear to be going smoothly on top, but one or two people who really wanted to live a life that would make them holy could be rather deceived about themselves, and get deceived about others, younger than themselves, coming in.

Think of Mother Mary of Jesus, the Carmelite who died in 1942 in the Notting Hill Carmel. She entered in Paris when she was young, and was quite popular at first, according to the account of her life which is privately published – I got a copy from the Carmel and subsequently gave my copy to R. D. Laing. Then she suddenly felt one day at communal recreation that she simply must get away and be alone. Well, you don't just walk off to your cell if you're in that situation, so she got a headache and was excused. She lay there for about two years. They got a doctor to her and a priest: one said that a beautiful butterfly would emerge from the chrysalis; and the other said if that were madness, would that all the world were mad. So somehow she must not have upset her superiors to the extent that it was [seen as] anti-social behaviour, and they accepted that she just had that need for that time.

Eventually, she took her place again in communal life, and when the then Cardinal in London wanted a Carmel founded, she was sent with a group of nuns from Paris and they founded the Carmel that's still there in Notting Hill. From there she went around the British Isles and founded more Carmelite convents than St Teresa of Avila founded in her day and age in Spain.

In some ways I think today there are more opportunities for lay people to retire for short periods, make a retreat, be alone, rather than giving their whole life [to a religious order]; and they're not so strict on the whole about vows in the Catholic Church today. People come out more easily – leave for good – without jumping over walls, if you understand me.

AS: I'm still not sure I'm clear about something. Let's see how I can put it. You opened up a very interesting issue around the strictness of routine functioning as a defence against the inner needs that one might have. We'd begun to talk about the way in which psychotherapy does something different from a religious order. I'd like to keep on that track. I'm wondering whether part of what you're getting at is that someone may wish to lead a religiously devout life, but be held back because they're full of unresolved, repressed anger or an unresolved inheritance from their childhood. Would you say that religious orders have difficulty in taking up those issues directly, but that psychotherapy as a form of practice takes that as its object of study, one might say?

MB: I think in theory no, if they have contact with a psychotherapist, but in practice yes. I think there are many Catholics who are trying to enter a religious order who, if they were told by someone from the order, 'I think you may well find fulfilment here, but really I think you should go to a psychotherapist for a short time first', would be very inclined to follow that advice. That would be for the good of the religious order and for the individual. Or if somebody who is already a nun has that need then, I think, it's a very good thing. Fortunately in Glasgow there is the Garnet Hill Centre, a Catholic non-residential psychotherapy unit, whose priest director is a Jesuit with medical cover.

I do think there is everything to be said for the appreciation of depth understanding, for student priests and nuns. Just as for medical students, or for psychiatrists who are doing the analytical training, I think a deep appreciation of this need is important. I always think, when I hear the prayer of St Francis – 'Lord that I may understand rather than be understood' – God help me if I wasn't *understood*. It's terribly important, when you consciously seek to get as fulfilled as you can here and now in this life.

AS: I'd be interested to see how you react to something that's been written by an analyst of the British Psycho-Analytical Society, Neville Symington. It's in a review of a book on the Mary cult which *Free Associations* will be publishing [Symington, 1989, in press]. He says: 'I have the distinct impression that many analysts are frightened of religion. I think one reason is that they are afraid to face the religious aspects of psychoanalysis itself. Another is that religious devotion, especially in its more intense forms, comes from the psychotic area of the personality, and many analysts are afraid to come to grips with this primitive area of the personality.' I'd like to focus on his suggestion that religious devotion comes from the psychotic area of the personality. My reason for sounding you out about this is that psychosis, in the way that you write about it in the book, suggests an area of experience that you need to go through, so to speak, in order to leave it behind.

MB: Yes.

AS: When you talk about 'having been mad' it suggests an experience that has been transcended.

MB: Yes.

AS: On the other hand, religious devotion can be something lifelong. Could there, pursuing this line of thought, ever be something psychotic *in* religious devotion, at source or by nature?

MB [*hesitating*]: . . . Religious devotion does consist, to quite a large extent, of attention to prayers that have been written by people of that particular religion. Now I think that the very young child, who is nearer than many older people to whence it has come – its soul – is in a state of freshness and innocence and natural longing that can get covered over as a person becomes more adult in years. Just as our body has physical needs in order to grow, so our non-physical part also has certain needs. You might say: yes, there are the mountains with the snow, there is the changing sky every day, and we see that and worship God and we appreciate it. An animal, a tree, just in its being, its growth, without doing anything, just by living, is expressing itself. We are much more complex than what are called lower forms of life. I think all human beings all over the world have certain needs of the soul, as needs of the body.

[*Pausing*] The psychotic area, I would say, is when the personality loses its purity, when it's a bit deformed, in some way. A person who is holy, and emotionally whole, can have religious experiences that might be termed mystical. Such people, however, are in touch with external reality and quite practical and sensible in the daily conduct of their lives. In fact, with the inner mystical experience can come a high degree of external practical application. My understanding of 'psychotic' is that it is an experience of a divorce from external reality. I'm not holy if I forget who I am, or if I see you as, for example, the King of England who has come to cut my throat – or the other crazy things that people say. In this state I'm a person in desperate need of analytical help to understand that such thoughts are fantasies and external projections of a very sick inner state. It is possible for a person to have a genuine vision of, for example, the Virgin Mary; that, to me, wouldn't be psychotic *because* the person would know who they were, where they were, and be able and continue to be able to behave in a manner that was perfectly acceptable to their fellow human beings. Psychosis, to me, is sickness. It could be a state or step on the way to holiness, but if the individual cannot come through it, he cannot become holy. Anything of a supernatural nature is built upon the natural.

AS: It sounds to me, on the question of the source of religious devotion, as if you wouldn't agree with Neville Symington's view. Your view might be rather that religious devotion simply exists, predating the individual – that it doesn't come from the individual personality, or from any one area within the personality.

MB: I think many people must have a sense of the divine within themselves, and whether they're working it out in terms of a primitive culture or whether they're in the Western world and say they are agnostic, I think they probably do have times in their lives when they instinctively turn to a higher being; perhaps when they're in grave danger or at the moment of death. Also, I think some people are given a certain amount of light and turn away from it. I think people who have followed evil impulses have turned from a possible light.

AS: Let's change direction a little, and focus on matters concerning psychotherapy and the practice of psychotherapy itself. I'm struck by how much we could still say about why regression is therapeutic. There are a number of questions that present themselves. I suppose one of the most obvious, because it's often raised, is whether it can be entered into in a way that can, as it were, wreak havoc rather than become a process of healing. Perhaps we could begin by speaking about how, in your view, the kind of deep regression you went through works.

MB: Yes, it's a very very individual matter to what extent the person may have denied themselves the expression of their true being, if very early on they had a lot of fear of doing something that might have offended their particular mother. I was brought up very clean, with a horror of my productions (at the beginning physical shits) – and I think it served a real purpose in my being able to go back to that level without a terrible feeling of guilt attached to it.

AS: Suppose you go back to that early experience – and I think there's an open question about whether one can ever truly 'go back' to an experience one has had, or feels that one had – of avoiding any kind of dirt because you're afraid of offending your mother; and supposing at Kingsley Hall you go back to that experience in spades, so to speak, and there's shit all over the walls. Do you discover then that you don't offend significant people, and is it that that's therapeutic?

MB [*laughing*]: Oh no, no! You discover that you do offend people, to a high degree.

AS [*laughing*]: That's rather what I was getting at.

MB: But you rediscover that your productions, even if they offend your mother, or other people, are not in themselves evil and wrong. And if you can have those baby shits, well then you might even produce a painting, and not feel a lot of guilt about it. (Somebody once said to me, 'Mary, you made money out of shit', when the book came out.) But the baby gets the wrong idea of its shit when it gets a lot of guilt about it. If a person can realize that in itself it's not a filthy thing to have a production, then with its creative ability later on – as it grows into a child that has a pencil, or clay – it doesn't have, firstly, a terrible fear of producing anything; and, secondly, a horror of this evil happening that's come out of it.

All right, it must learn not to stay producing shit all its life; it must move on. So a reasonable balance must be attained, even with a real baby. But if you hadn't repressed it so much and wanted it to produce to order, before its sphincter muscles were capable of producing shit into a pot – if you hadn't tried to force undue cleanliness too soon – then it would be in a better situation to move on naturally from shit to acceptable creative things for other people.

AS: I suspect that many people who are in more conventional forms of therapy are working on and trying to work through these kinds of experiences, but still verbally. It leads me to wonder about the balance between verbal interpretation within a session, and the reliving of experience. I can see one could come to something tangible about creativity by going through the kind of regression that you're describing: it seems to make possible a process of recapitulation. But I still want to know if you think it can in certain circumstances be harmful.

MB: I would think it's harmful to cling to it, to prolong it unnecessarily, and very dangerous to get lost in it. I think it is very important that a person alone does not try to go through a regression without skilled help.

AS: I'm also interested in the other forms of therapy that you've hinted at when we've talked, one of which is underwater diving. That, if I understood you, was a way of reliving a birth experience –

MB: And a prebirth experience.

AS: I'd like to tease out a bit how you see that as therapeutic.

MB: Yes. I do think, whether the experience is talked about or not, especially when people are in analytical situations, it can be quite powerful therapy: the feeling of it, rather than the talking about it. I'm well aware that some people in the course of an analytical session go through an experience of birth. But there would seem to be some people who could talk it all out with an analyst and completely understand it in the head or the intellect; but not have as much real emotional change as they might have, for example, if they'd shut up and felt it.

I'm not suggesting, by any means – and I do have to say this again, when we talk about households for the Shealin Trust – that it's not envisaged that people will go around putting shit on the walls. I had a very long and unusual experience, and I don't necessarily think that is necessary to the majority of people having any psychotherapeutic or analytical help. And also, I think that when it happens, it can serve its purpose and finish; you don't do it for the rest of your life. It needn't be so publicly spread about, as it were; some people may have such experiences, but in a much more limited and private way.

So I think that regression has a part to play in healing. Sometimes people are trying to play that part in conventional mental hospitals, but there's no analyst to pick it up, so it's not used in a good way. I guess I ended up in a chronic ward, in a padded cell in the dark, curled up like a foetus, because I wanted to go back to before I was born; probably because I felt comparatively safe within the uterus and I had a lot of fear about the birth. My mother would have done too, as we were both three days and three nights in labour. I was premature and there were terrible conflicts, I think, ending up with whether I was going to live or die.

AS: What's very interesting there is that the impulse is going to be to return to a place of safety –

MB: Yes –

AS: – and the uterus has the quality of a place of safety – but I'm remembering in one of our earlier conversations that you said, 'Coming up isn't usually a problem; going down is more of a problem.' It seems to me there is perhaps a paradox there because the regressive impulse is going to be to *stay* in that place of safety. Whereas I also know, from our conversations, that coming up is what's needed. Can there not be quite a tension between the sense of where the place of safety is and the need to come up, and return to the social world of everyday experience?

MB [*animated*]: Oh yes, yes, and it can happen over and over again. I went up and down several times in Kingsley Hall. Although it's comparatively easy to come up, you can still have fears about it. That period of ambivalence is not necessarily bad. You need time to get into the water, or to get out of the water. I can see a goodness about ambivalence, and for that matter compromise. Overall, I do feel very much there's the timing of God: meeting the right person at the right time, being in the right place at the right time.

AS: I know that you acknowledge the need for skill and training in psychotherapy, and I know that you take the view that someone who has been helped may then be of use to others. I remember being struck by your saying that you would never hit someone

– 94 –

whom you didn't see as a therapist; it suggests that you recognize that there is something in the *role* of the therapist which is different from the role of a companion or a member of a peer group. If the person is a therapist then they are there to take one's projected bad stuff, do something with it and give it back to you in a more digested form.

MB: I think now that I was probably referring to times when I was very afraid to express anger and afraid of hurting a person, but I can also imagine that there could be times when, in an ordinary sense, I just get a bad temper and I could easily hit a child, for example, if I was in a parent situation; whether I was the real blood-mother or not. If I was in a mother or teacher's situation and that child was annoying me, I could well imagine giving it a good shake and I wouldn't have seen it as a therapist at all [*laughs*]! I am so well aware of how badly you can damage a child emotionally as well as physically by hitting it. I can also see that if I didn't really physically damage it, I might not have hurt it so much as if I'd kept nag, nag, nagging at it. There are things that are worse than a hit to a child, which is not the same as *advocating* physical punishment for children.

AS: When you say, as you do, that one hour of therapy is never wasted, what do you think goes on in that one hour that is different from . . . .

MB: ordinary life . . . ?

AS: Well, yes, from ordinary life.

MB: The person is before another human being who is trying, solely, for that period of time, to really understand them. That is a circumstance that would be very rare to find outside the therapist's session. You might find something akin in terms of [the relationship of] a novice to a spiritual director; however, the spiritual director would really, in terms of spiritual direction or analytical knowledge, have to have the same knowledge [of texts] in order to be able to really help them. The very fact that two people are spending that time in trying to understand the problems of one of the two cannot help but be helpful to the person who has sought that help, for example in the co-counselling situation. I really think that.

As to the therapeutic relationship [*hesitating*] . . . Ronnie Laing says, 'Life is therapy, and therapy is life.' But within the confines of the practice of psychotherapy, there are – and I think quite rightly so – definite lines to try to keep roughly within, because it's not like an ordinary social relationship, it's at a much deeper level.

AS: I would put this in the context of the concept of transference, which also focuses on the way in which the person who is in therapy is projecting on to their analyst sets of patterns –

MB: Yes –

AS: Which were laid down in relation to their own parents –

MB: Yes –

AS: And which may be keeping them stifled, or unwell.

MB: Right. The therapeutic relationship is a relationship that enables them to recall those forces that are rather overpowering them in their life, and to play them out towards the therapist. Through the getting of them out and the understanding of them – letting air, fresh air, as it were, in to their own souls – they can then become able, from trusting the therapist, to trust themselves. And so live, fully themselves, when they no longer have the need of that relationship. And it's the therapist who largely determines that timing.

AS: You have also talked of the great love that you were able to feel for your parents at the end of their lives. I couldn't help wondering about the possibility of a positive idealization after all the years of anger and hatred and difficulty. I guess my starting point there would be the assumption that one always feels ambivalent about significant others, particularly family members. I would be unhappy with a move from 'the anger' to the great love, as though one then has only positive feelings, one then has only loving or harmonious relationships. There are situations in which people, however hard they work therapeutically, or however hard they come to terms with their own history, remain uncomfortable with their parents, feel deeply let down. Their experience of therapy cannot necessarily compensate for that.

I just wanted to clarify whether when you speak about the great love that it becomes possible to feel if you've had therapy, that doesn't necessarily exclude continuing to feel the letdown or the disappointment?

MB: Yes, one doesn't forget the bad things. I feel that one is very aware that it is not for oneself to judge or to bear a grudge, and one positively can feel a great love and compassion, because you can see how tied up they are and how they really were trying to do the best they could, as they saw it at the time.

That doesn't mean to say that when, historically, you look back over the time that certain things went very wrong, that you feel any different. But I do think forgiveness is also involved, if you feel that on a practical level something definitely seemed a wrong step that might have been avoided (like when my brother was put to a different school, and it affected his life very much).

I found in my personal experience that I really did feel love and compassion. I felt also that I wouldn't have wanted to go over the past; I wanted to let it rest. Also I was aware of a lot of goodness that had happened through my particular experience that couldn't have happened if I'd had a much different upbringing. I'm all for good soil to put plants in, but you can put a plant in good soil and it can die; you can put a plant almost just on a rock in a tiny bit of soil and it flourishes. There is something beyond what you can really fully comprehend in all this.

AS: You're involved in establishing a psychotherapeutic household. Let me ask what, for you, makes a good psychotherapist.

MB: According to their state of emotional maturity they need individual analytical help, to concentrate on gaining greater maturity in themselves. Apart from that they need an appreciation of the struggles of other people, so that they have a sympathetic attitude. Over and above all, they need a conscious awareness of the healing power of love.

According to how much the therapist feels in themselves that they can bear to read and study at certain times, then that is good. I think particular things are relevant. You remind me now that last May when I was in Norway, I was staying in the house of an analyst. There were books in English and, as I said, I was reading Bruno Bettelheim because Maria [the hospitalized young woman in Stockholm] had asked me to walk behind her on one occasion. The bit that I noticed about space made me feel how important it is, if you have impulses to hit, that you have your own space and that people are not too much on top of you. You can feel a fear of other human contacts onto you physically. That seemed important to me at the time that I read it.

I think that everyone's experience probably causes them to read particular things in books at particular times. At other times they apply what they've read and studied when the relevant subject is practically put before them in the behaviour of the person they're trying to help.

AS: But, in that psychotherapy can open up such dark areas of the personality, I think that a therapist needs the support, or back-up of structure, or containment, of a training organization.

MB [*animated*]: Yes, yes, right, I absolutely agree with you. Yes, yes, of course. I do think that there must be some criteria by which the lay people can judge whether the therapist is competent or not. I also think it's very important for the therapist to have group contact, because people are much better helped when the therapist isn't absolutely isolated with their problems with clients. Knowledge expands and grows because it's discussed. Supervision is very important. And also, from the point of view of the therapist's anxiety load it's essential.

AS: So that anxiety – elicited by the work, the stress of the work – has to be contained by someone else as well . . .

MB: Exactly . . .

AS: Metabolized, processed . . .

MB: Yes. For the good of the therapist's own survival. One has to have points of contact with others.

AS: Would this be one of the reasons why, when people have written to you, you have urged them to find a therapist for themselves, because you don't feel it would be appropriate for you to become that significant a figure for someone?

MB: I've always felt it was very important for me to be involved with the *housing* side of it more. There's lots of people training to be therapists, and there's lots of people needing therapy. There's comparatively few that go into special residential accommodation when they go into psychotherapy. For me, the importance of having somewhere to live at that time was not *more* important than having a therapist – I had to have the other side of it – but the living situation *was* very important. Also, with the painting and the writing, and my ageing physical years, I felt not strongly drawn to what I saw mainly as office therapy. I don't want to belittle that in any way, but that was how my life, individually, seemed to develop.

All right, the usual way is to go through some sort of therapy training and be part of a group. I have had the freedom and time – because I haven't had a book with a lot of appointments in it – to be much longer with individual people at certain periods. At times it's been a very intense relationship, but a *short* one – I'm thinking now of Roger, whom I cared for when he was regressed; it doesn't happen very often. All right, I haven't got money from a lot of appointments, but one way and another, I manage. It seems to suit my particular circumstances. I appreciate being able to be flexible, and go here and there; to meet somebody or to give a talk, because I think the educational side of this is very important. I am not myself a professional therapist, but I do feel a great desire to put those in need in touch with a psychotherapist. In a nutshell, I would say that over the years, whereas some people would say they've had patients and some have clients, I just have friends.

NOVEMBER 1988

1 *Tree*, the door of my room, Kingsley Hall, 1968

2   Chagford, front door, 1976

3 Scroll of the *Hollow Tree*, St Andrews, 1987

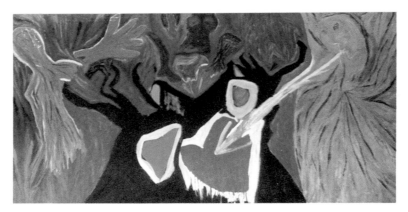

4 *Disintegration*, Kingsley Hall, April 1966

5 *The Temptation of Christ*, Kingsley Hall, April 1966

6 *Resurrection*, Kingsley Hall, July 1967

7 *The Ascension*, Kingsley Hall, September 1967

8   *Time of the Tomb*, Kingsley Hall, 1969

9   *Christ Carrying the Cross*, St Andrews, 1968

10 *The Mother of God or Break Through* (with Christ breaking as it were through a wall), Kingsley Hall, March 1968

11 *Our Lady of Africa*, finger painting, Kingsley Hall, May 1968

12 *Peter the Fisherman*, finger painting, Kingsley Hall, November 1968

PART 2
Writings

LIFE

For 'Angie' of the Play*

She says my name,
      Softly, gently,
Mary behind,
      Mary in front,
We – are complete
We gasp with relief
All the people are 'with us'.
There is Love and Peace,
Like a babe asleep
The play fades –
To the arms of the night
And the Dark
Its life doth hold –
As a Star,
      Embedded in
           Time

1979

---

* Judy Monahan played Angie in the Birmingham and Royal Court, London, productions of David Edgar's play *Mary Barnes*.

SUCCESS
For 'Mary'*

That you may on your winged way go,
    Fly high –
Soar to the stars,
    And in the light of the moon,
    Kiss thou –
    This dear earth –
    Mother of thy flesh,
    And lover of thy soul.
Play to the Sun –
Dance in the waves.
And in the shelter of thy Heart,
Do thou, in secret adoration,
    Bend to the
        applause of God
    For thy Breath and Being.

1979

---

* For Patti Love who played me.

DEATH OF A FAMILY

One day, a little boy went to see his Mother, who was sick, in bed, and because her heart was weak, she fainted when he hugged her hard.

He thought she was dead and that he had killed her and he was so frightened that he ran away and lived in a hollow tree in the wood, with a squirrel.

Above them in a nest lived their friend, the bird. One day the bird saw the little boy's Mother through the window of her house. She had been in hospital, in a bed with a temperature chart, but now she had returned.

He told the little boy, she is still alive. The little boy ventured back to the house.

His Mother was in a storm of anger, at his going away, and she hit the little boy so hard that he died.

When the Father came home, he was terrified and he ran out in a panic to telephone the doctor.

On the way, he fell into a hole in the road and was killed.

It seems they were all killed by fear. The little boy feeling his love had killed his Mother, was very frightened and ran away. Going later, in trust to his Mother, he is killed by her fear and grief and love, turned to anger.

The Father was 'beside himself' and ran into his death.

THE BUTTERFLY
AND THE SUN

There was once a beautiful red butterfly who went
about between the flowers delivering their letters for
them.

One day the Sunflower who was very proud and
tall, said,

'Butterfly, I want you to take this letter, quickly,
it is express delivery, to my friend, His Majesty, the
Sun. You see, it has his head on the stamp, and it
says O.H.M.S. On His Majesty's Service. It is very
important.'

The butterfly took the letter on her back. It was
heavy and she felt frightened, for she was not sure
of the way. She started upwards and a big black cloud
before her, opened his doors and poured forth his rain
all over her. She fell to the ground, drenched and
cold, and trembling in fear. There she lay, until she
felt the flutter of wings. It was the Angel of the Moon,
waking from her sleep of day. She said,

'Butterfly, come on my back, I know where the Sun
lives.'

So the butterfly went with the letter and the Angel
of the Moon, up to the Sun.

When they reached him, he was asleep for it was
night. He did not want to be disturbed, he said,

'It is not time for me to come out.'

The butterfly said,

'Please, your Majesty, I have a very important letter from your friend, the Sunflower.'

The Sun said,

'I am cross that she so bothers me', and opening one eye, he said,

'Butterfly *you* are very beautiful.' The butterfly moved her wings. The Sun opened his other eye.

He tore open the letter and he said,

'Butterfly, take this note back at once to the Sunflower. It says I shall not shine upon her unless *you* are resting on her head.'

The butterfly flew off, and reaching the Sunflower, her wings fluttering in fear, she delivered the letter of the Sun.

The Sunflower was indeed in a furious temper, but she knew if the Sun did not shine on her, she would die, so she had to obey, and she bent her head low, and the butterfly rested on her petals, and such then was the warmth of the sun that they both fell drowsily asleep in the heat of his love.

The Sun found a new lover. The butterfly found she was loved. The Sunflower found she had to share.

SUNFLOWER LAND

Miriam yawned, it was a warm sunny afternoon.
A big Sunflower opened wide his head and Miriam
slipped in, and down a stream of sap through the
tunnel of its stem into the dark warm earth. A worm
took her hand and lead her through a mountain of
stones into a castle called 'Root Hall'.

There she lingered in a maze of Hollows, lit by
glow-worms in a network of gold. She picked some
filaments, filled the pockets of her dress, and emerged
to catch the Rabbit Express.

Through burrows warm with fur, the Rabbit carried
her up to the Day, and there, he left her sitting on
the grass.

You go *down*, slipping in fluid
You go *through*, a mountain.
You *linger*, in gold, and pick your fill.
You are carried *up* and Out.

THE HOLLOW TREE*

There was once a tree in the forest who felt very sad
and lonely for her trunk was hollow and her head was
lost in mist. Sometimes, the mist seemed so thick that
her head felt divided from her trunk. To the other
trees she appeared quite strong but rather aloof, for
no wind ever bent her branches to them. She felt if
she bent she would break yet she grew so tired of
standing straight. So it was with relief that, in a
mighty storm, she was thrown to the ground. The tree
was split, her branches scattered, her roots torn up
and her bark was charred and blackened.

She felt stunned, and thought her head was clear
of the mist she felt her sap dry as she felt her deadness
revealed when the hollow of her trunk was open to
the sky. The other trees looked down and gasped and
didn't quite know whether to turn their branches
politely away or whether to try to cover her emptiness
and blackness with their green and brown. The tree
moaned for her own life and feared to be suffocated
by theirs. She felt she wanted to lay bare and open
to the wind and the rain and the sun, and that, in time,
she would grow up again, full and brown from the
ground. So it was, that, with the wetness of the rain,
she put down new roots and by the warmth of the
sun she stretched forth new wood.

In the wind her branches bent to other trees and
as their leaves rustled and whispered, in the dark and
in the light, the tree felt loved and laughed with life.

---

* Written as a birthday present for R. D. Laing.

THE MIRACLE OF MARY
A Baby Bear Story for Michael*

There was once a Big Bear whose native environment
was the land of North America. He ventured far
away, into the jungle of England. There, in a special
part of the jungle, it was somewhat enclosed, like a
nursery for seedlings, he met a baby bear. Her colour
kept changing. Sometimes she was transparent. He
could see right through her. He knew she saw what
she looked at, though she looked as if she didn't see.
What she had, she hid. He wanted to see what she
had. She had shits and weird noises and long hair.
Sometimes she came out at night, prowling about to
see what was left after the other animals had fed. She
burrowed away, he got to helping her make holes.
She was going down, to grow up.

When the Big Bear came close, she let him feed
her, then she thought she was inside him. She tried
to take his colour. The Big Bear didn't like her smell,
he had his own shit. However, he was out to explore,
and to preserve the wild life of the jungle. Carefully,
so as not to frighten her away he continued to hold
out food for her. Sometimes she fed, then would go
'all away' as if she had no right to be there, being
as one of an 'extinct species'. Yet she tried to survive.
Her habits didn't seem to conform to those of the
other animals. They felt she was dangerous, and

---

* Michael Dempsey, editor of *Mary Barnes: Two
Accounts of a Journey Through Madness.*

wanted to turn her out from the special enclosure, to
wander alone in the vast jungle.

Big Bear ran to her protection and as he had the
jaws of a crocodile, and the teeth of a shark, the other
animals soon swam away. Sometimes Baby Bear spun
a web, like a spider, then she would hibernate as if
frozen into an iceberg. Yet she was not a white polar
bear, nor yet a black bear. She loved Fire. Her species
was obscure. Yet, she liked Honey, so she was a
Bear. Big Bear, licking honey off his paws, would
give a pad for her to suck. Sometimes she'd twist into
a heap, as if she'd rather die than eat.

In the past they'd tried to tame her, and once she'd
been shut up in the Zoo, a place where rare specimens
were preserved. The keepers had white coats. She'd
wanted one.

Big Bear sought to show her how to live in different
places, like he did. She felt if she undid her lock she
would explode into oblivion. Yet all her life was
bursting out. Big Bear thought maybe *she can paint*.

Meanwhile, from the mist and bogs of Ireland, by
the hand of Patrick and the Holy Ghost, a dark Bear
was emerging from his lair. He came stalking in the
jungle. Unloosing traps and snares, he saw every evil
that was there. Snakes he thrust into the ground and
when Big Bear cried in battle Michael was there to
clear the air.

Baby Bear, safely in her lair, was making pictures,
with paint and papers, wood and canvas. Big Bear
got them hung in an exhibition, so she got recognition.

Michael from the land of green bears, wondered
what this rainbow was. He thought, maybe she can
paint in words. Big Bear told her, you can growl,
you lick and sniff, and paint with shit. You can put
the world in words.

Big Bear was very pleased, because without

'catching' Baby Bear he had saved her from
extinction. She was so free, she danced with glee.

Together, they wrote all about it. Michael, moving
to another cave, took with him all that they had made.
There he cooked it to a book, and when all was set
and served, Baby Bear leapt with delight for the
'colour' was just right.

Her coat shone with health and vigour. Big Bear
had brushed out all the tangles.

Now some new fur they got for Michael.
From food so long prepared,
    My souls and bodies,
        meet in
          God.

FEAST OF ST MICHAEL ARCHANGEL
SEPTEMBER 1971.

PROJECTIONS

I feel I'm dying
Are you dead?
I love you dearly
Shall you kiss me?

Why don't you respond
You are me:

I feel you
What have I done
That *you* are so bad?

I'm furious with me
Why don't *you* scream?

I hate myself
Why are you killing yourself?

Don't be jealous of me
Because I envy you.

Let's untie the knot
And feel for ourselves.

MY FRIENDS

My Friends –
How they devour me,
biting off chunks of
my flesh, which with
relish, they chew, spitting
the crunched up bones
onto my soul, and still
I LOVE them, for they
are my Friends.

VOYAGE OF MY SOUL

Door – to door,
And not sure whether to go,
Leaning back toward heaven,
The inevitable push –
I fought free –
Alright don't speed
The rush of death –
Is but of Breath.
Wait, take it easy
No need to fight –
The flight to light.

Conceived at moment of movement:
Timeless space before the flight –
From everlasting light,
To be entombed in seed of life,
Soul, caught in web of Flesh to be.
Entering life,
As a Bird in flight:
Till back, into the nest of heaven,
From Light to Dark,
And back to brilliance of everlasting
Dawn.

SANCTITY

Sancity is Love, of the height and width and depth of God.

Sanctity is unity. It is madness to be divided from God, cut off from the Holy Spirit within.

The desire for God is the desire for Indivisibility and sanctity is letting God bring one to it.

At the end of the world will complete unity be achieved. My flesh, my body reunited with my soul.

Beyond this life will my soul wait.

Here and now dwelling in my flesh, the sacred temple of Christ, does my soul taste of ultimate completeness, and in so doing, it leans forward towards its flight.

GETHSEMANI

'Father, if thou wilt, remove this chalice from me; but yet not my will, but thine be done.' (LUKE 22:42)

The most gentle, the most violent, the most *sensational* life is feeling towards its suffering, to death. Yet, in its agony is it held, in balance.

The possibility of release, yet the decision to retain.

Over and over again the enduring moment of soul torment has groaned to let go, yet persistently held.

For the WILL to relinquish the WILL, is strong beyond all human bounds.

The Love that *is* GOD is moving nearer the CROSS.

The imminent torture is the pinnacle of the climb of humanity to the light of heaven.

The journey foreshadowed from the seed of Adam to the birth of Christ, fashioned by GOD to lift MAN back unto Himself, is the Via del a Rosa all who will may tread.

The path one is invited to go.

To those who seek GOD will give, not by force but in Love. Through a Love that flees the flesh, is sustained by the Angels, and rests in GOD its source and fulfilment.

MOVEMENT

God, in a tiny seed, planted Himself, by the Holy
Spirit, in the womb of Mary.

The seed falls into the ground. It splits open, it
divides, and it pushes up through the womb of the
earth, and is revealed.

> GOD is as the sun, warm and opening:
> GOD is as the cold, stringent and exhilarating;
> GOD is as the light, revealing.
> GOD is as the rain, cool and refreshing.
> GOD is as the dryness, a thirst to the earth.
> GOD is as the wind, breath of the lungs of the
> world.

All that receives, gives.

The womb receives the seed, and it opens and
gives. The soul receives the word of God and it gives
God. The light of day is as a shadow compared with
the light of God in the soul.

The soul is lost and found in God. It becomes as
water, seeping through the soil, as lightning streaking
through the sky, as thunder rumbling in the night, as
a *star*, shining in the orbit of God.

As the seed grows and flowers and ripens so it sheds
its seeds and all creation is increased and God is
blessed in the birth of new life.

All creation is of God and of its being loves God

and in all the movement of all its life is drawn to
God.

God, in coming to earth as the seed, in the womb,
divided and multiplied Himself in growth, and after
His death He gave His very flesh and blood for
division and multiplication among men.

In the perpetual sacrifice and communion of Christ
in the world, is the redemption, the salvation of
mankind.

Just as the seed splits and divides and multiplies
in growth so does the soul. The Holy Spirit, the power
of God, in the soul stretches forth, as a light, as a
word, as love.

Through the light of the soul is revealed, meaning:
and in the shrouded mystery of night, as in the tomb
before the resurrection, the soul cleaves to God, and
is lost, in Him who, *is*; the meaning of all things;
in secret and in mystery is God revealed. In light and
in darkness is He seen, and as a fish moving in deep
water He stirs the depths of the soul.

As a fish finds food in the weed, so is the soul
consumed by Christ. In its many strands of being is
the food of God. Only God, who put it there, knows
just where to find it; and as the soul, in the seeking
of the Fish, is split into God, so is it nourished and
fulfilled.

As is the Mother given unto and fulfilled by the
sucking of the babe.

PASSION

Shrinks the flesh
From the Passion of Christ
Twisted in agony
Soul bent and torn
Bruised, battered and worn

– Is the Body Divine
Caught in that moment
                 of Time
When was sealed
                 through flesh
The Sting of His Spirit to
                 Man
So now – in the Passion
                 of Love
Do we the flesh consume
Crucified Life
Set to the Sea
Of everlasting
               Light.

THE CROSS OF CHRIST
A News Story – How God moves

I was a stranger in Jerusalem and unaware of the
recent happenings.

I heard loud shouting and saw a huge mob and
amidst the noise there arose loud screams, as of
wolves howling for blood, and the howl was of the
words,

'Crucify Him',
'Crucify Him'.

I wondered who Him was. A woman beside me,
silent and tense, whispered,

'He forgave me my sins, and my brother, who had
been dead four days, He brought to life.'

I moved away from her, not that she looked exactly
mad, but such strange words unnerved my mind. I
wanted to be on my way, back to the quiet of the
country, yet I lingered, horribly fascinated.

It became quieter, Pilate was washing his hands.

I edged nearer and spoke with a soldier. He said,

'It's a queer business. When in Galilee I met a
fellow called Peter – can't see him around today –
but he told me, once when they were in a boat and
there was a great storm, Jesus suddenly brought the
wind and the water to utter stillness.'

I'd like to believe it, what they say about Him, –
but – 'Look, there He is'. The soldier pulled me to
a forward position.

They were leading a man out of a building. He

looked completely alone, and with a strange sadness, smiled, as if in His fear, He had an unknown peace.

I longed to come closer. I crept away from the soldier and bent low to the ground.

Suddenly, I was on my face on the ground, knocked down by the beam of a great Cross they were causing Him to carry.

I stretched out my hand and I touched Him.

Stumbling back into the crowd I was lost to all but Him and I was bent up in myself, with a knowledge beyond all words.

THE SHEPHERD

For myself – for all who came to Kingsley Hall. 'Whosoever loveth this life shall lose it.'

It was the eve of the Sabbath. I had that day been to the temple. Words of Isaiah, in odd phrases, were racing through my mind; 'He shall feed his flock – like a shepherd.' How was God going to feed us? There had been bread, manna, in the desert. 'He shall grow up, as a tender plant . . . A root out of a thirsty ground . . . Despised and abject of *men* . . . His look was as it were hidden . . . Bruised for our sins . . . Shall be led as a sheep to the slaughter . . . The Lord of Hosts is his name . . . Eat that which is good' . . . and . . . 'Your soul shall be delighted in fatness . . . All you that thirst come to the waters.'

I yawned, it was really too cold for sleep. I stretched my legs and felt the warmth of the sheep. There seemed something strange about the air. The sheep were unsettled. Nathaniel and David moved over to me. We sat huddled together. I became wrapped in prayer. We seemed lost in the deep darkness of the night.

Suddenly, I saw a light, a great streak stretching from the heavens of the sky, and it widened, and the whole earth was enlightened. We trembled in fear and lay upon the ground, and I heard the words, 'Fear not, for behold I bring you good tidings of great joy that shall be to all the people. For this day is born to you a saviour, who is Christ, the Lord, in the City of David. And this shall be a sign unto you. You shall find the infant wrapped in swaddling clothes and laid in a manger.'

I looked up, *and* towering above me was an angel. And other angels came, saying, 'Glory to God in the highest, and on earth peace to men of good will.'

Then suddenly, it was dark again, completely quiet and still. I felt the sheep settle. David was rubbing his eyes. I knew it was no dream. I felt quite certain, it was the Messiah. At that moment I *knew* God had come to earth.

We went, to the City of David, to Bethlehem. We knew we wanted to go and we went quickly. There, with a man named Joseph, and a woman, Mary, was an Infant, in a manger, and him we adored, knowing him to be the Lord.

We came back, quietly, in awe, yet in great peace. Later, I heard, Kings from the East had come to Bethlehem, and then, on the orders of Herod, all the male children of Bethlehem, under two years, were slain.

I tended to keep to myself that which I knew; though all were aware in the anger and grief of the mothers, that Herod must have been given cause for such a violence. Nothing was said in the Temple I went to, and somehow just then, I did not feel inclined to speak, where I felt I would be doubted.

For some years nothing more was heard, then Herod died; and one day I was taking some sheep into Galilee, I came to Nazareth. I was thirsty and tired and went towards a well. There was a woman drawing water and her eyes dwelt upon me. I knew her to be the Mother of Christ, and I felt she remembered me. I said, 'How is he, the Son of God?'

She smiled and gave me some water and bade me,
'Come and see.'

She led me along a narrow street and we entered
a house through the workshop of a carpenter. I smelt
the wood; there, beside Joseph, I saw Him, the Son
of God. 'Jesus,' said his mother, 'Bring a chair for
the shepherd, he has come again, to see you.'
Bringing a chair, He went again for water, and He
washed my feet. The sight of Mary was upon me.

It was some time before I saw Him again. I was
a shepherd, and the sheep of my pastures knew my
hand. The country was quiet, in my local temple
nothing was heard of Him. It seemed the Son of God,
the Messiah, was passing unnoticed and unknown. I
remembered the words of Isaiah, 'His look was as
it were, hidden.'

Then, there was the business of John the Baptist.
Christ went to him to be baptized in the Jordan, and
John knew Him from afar to be the Son of God.

From then on, the whole country was astir, with
the news of Jesus. He started preaching; He was now
a man of thirty years; He did miracles; He forgave
sins; crowds followed Him; He was 'news', there was
no longer anywhere, any peace and quiet.

Some people were angry, especially some priests
of the temple; many were happy, especially the sick
He healed. I was thrilled and caught up in the
excitement of the time. I heard Him say, 'I am the
living bread He that eateth my flesh and drinketh my
blood abideth in me and I in him.'

It seemed I didn't then know how; that this was
the way He was to 'feed His flock'; rather than
perhaps by many multiplications of loaves and fishes.
I felt the heavenly mystery, as when I heard the
Angel, and first saw Him, as a babe.

Another time, I was in a crowd, and I thought it

was Him, Jesus Christ. I got near. He was talking in parables to the multitudes. He seemed to see me, yet was not looking towards me. He went on talking, to the crowd, and picking a bud from the vine, He bent towards me, and His attention seemingly not diverted, He yet spoke these words, to me alone, almost in a whisper, 'As I picked this bud so also will I clutch you,' and he gave me the bud. I quickly moved away, secreting the bud, as the greatest treasure I could ever know.

So it went on, the stir, the miracles; He brought Lazarus back from the dead. For three years He was seen, He was heard, He was loved; yet some were very jealous of His power, and denied He was the son of God. He was mocked, and scourged, and crucified. 'Led as a sheep to the slaughter, bruised for our sins.'

I was part of it all. I am of His flesh and blood, of His race. I have lived in His time, the time that was for ever on the horizon of our Fathers. For generations God carried us towards the fulfilment of the promise of Himself. It was so beautiful, stupendous as lightning, and yet so simple, like grass growing, that many passed by, 'walked over him', without ever knowing.

He was not long a prisoner. They very quickly crucified Him. I found my way there, to where He was hanging, near a thief, and He whispered to him, 'This day thou shalt be with me in paradise.' The words cut through my soul and I watched and waited until there was darkness over all the land, and the whole earth seemed to be breaking to pieces.

I saw His body taken from the cross. I knew he rose from the dead, three days later; and when He ascended into heaven, I was in the fields, with my sheep.

I am in prison now. I was taken by Saul, and bound in chains. I am afraid, yet I will not deny Christ. I know, for it has been given me to know. I cannot have much longer to live. Those words of Christ I heard, heard with my own ears, 'This day thou shalt be with me in paradise', those words keep hammering, hammering, in my soul. I clutch the bud He gave me when He said to me, 'As I picked this bud so also will I clutch you.' It is still in the pocket of my cloak. I was searched, but no thought was taken of this. They will kill my body, yet I shall be with Him in paradise; as the bud of the vine, I shall fruit in Him. Lord, I am not worthy. That night, the night you came, the angels, 'Glory to God in the highest', the Crucifixion, your hands that healed; that crown of thorns, Mary Magdalen, the forgiveness of sins – Lord, I am not worthy. 'Whosoever shall eat my flesh and drink my blood', I heard you say it; the Ascension, the Holy Spirit, God the Father, God the Son.

Oh God, God, help me to die as you did. 'Father forgive them for they know not what they do.' God, God, *forgive* Saul, and tell him, *tell* him. God, take me, *take* me and *tell* Saul. God, *please God – tell* Saul.

Epilogue

On his way to Damascus, to hound Christians, Saul was blinded, by God, for three days. He changed his name to Paul. With Peter, Saint Paul is especially honoured on June 29th.

Oh yes, God *did* tell Saul.

RESURRECTION

In the night the Body of Christ moved into life.

Bound in a winding sheet Lazarus stepped from the grave. The daughter of Jairus returned to life, and Peter, after the Ascension of Christ, raised up Tabitha from death. Elias laid upon the child and his life returned.

At the Fall, when man was mutilated in love, cut off from God, received the possibility of sin and the physical fact of death, there was the resurrection. As man moved away from God so was he retrieved.

The moment the leaf falls, there is the Spring. In the depths of being, is all knowing.

To live the present is to reap the past and sow the future.

Man is split, entombed, and resurrected.

Born again, of the Spirit, of water, as a spring, bursting up from caverns of the soul, as rain finding its way out again.

As flesh from bone becomes new ground, so into life breaks new birth.

In the night a babe was born: in the morn the resurrected Christ walked forth, from human flesh. The Trinity in transition in the Son, yet ever one. In the womb, as in the tomb, God in hidden darkness lay.

Angels paved the way – 'The Holy Spirit shall come upon thee and the power of the most High shall overshadow thee' –

Mary carried the Child, and He went on before.

– 'He is not here: He has gone on' – The tomb
deserted, as an empty womb, as the nest when birds
migrate. Time to move, to change, to live in other
forms – 'Touch me not, I have not yet ascended to
my Father' –

Touch not the bud till the sheath be open.

In His going was His coming. Yet last year's leaf
is not this year's bud.

From the root of Jesse, from the womb of Mary,
through the Cross from out the tomb, He came.

In resurrected glory rose. – 'Lo I am with you
always' –

In all ways, through all days, the Light Isaiah knew
abides.

– 'A light shall shine upon us this day: for the lord
is born to us: and He shall be called Wonderful, God,
the Prince of Peace, the Father of the world to come:
of whose reign there shall be no end.' –

Words beyond time, flashes of love in the power
of God.

From Calvary, into the Catacombs, and up to the
moon, time moves as the sky, changing with the wind
and clouds, yet ever held, in the mind of God.

Life, teeming as an ant hill, sparse as grass in
drought, dying as a day; rises with the moon, to shed
new light upon the earth.

6 NOVEMBER, 1970

THE RESOLUTION OF ANGER

Before the spoken word is anger resolved. Saint
John tells us – 'I will make you pure, as Christ' –

Mother Mary of Jesus, years before the birth of
thirty-three convents, lay alone in her cell, not
physically ill. In the depths of her being was
knowledge of the time to come. Unable to be involved
in anything outside herself, she was paving the way
for her work to be, was resolving anger, softening
the earth to receive new plants.

They grew, bore fruit. In the frail 'foolishness of
Christ', is the wisdom, the strength, that takes into
itself the festering poison. The wound is sucked, the
sore is healed. The sponge absorbs, dissolves; it is
dry. We are the oil of the world making easy the way.

The lock is turned, the door is open, God is
revealed. The wall caves in, no longer can the truth
be hid. The anger is resolved, the binding barrier
broken, as in the soft warm flesh of life is felt the
love, anger in hardness tried to conceal.

O, Mother of God, thy breasts are of infinite
tenderness. What love in thy milk. It runs as a stream
in the desert, drunk by the hungry hearts of men.

We are parched to cry with tears of compassion to
melt the wax in each other's souls. To kneel at the
feet of Thy Son in worship, to rest as a babe in the
lap of God. To be – 'delivered from evil' – from all
guilt, that kills and clogs and bars from God.

– 'Lamb of God who takest away the sins of the world, grant us peace' – The peace of being at rest in God, lying awake in love. Of knowing the world, from within the soul.

The tent is open, the cloud has passed, warm sun melts the ice, anger is resolved. New life is born, someone gets free, the bird is let be, we peer in the nest in awe; anger is resolved.

The mystery of life, the birth of Christ, the perfume of a rose, red in colour, bleeding as His wounds, pulls the supple soul to God. Freed from hard knots, tormenting twists and bands of steel, the soul in the arms of God doth sleep, lulled into the life of light. No longer groping in the dark, as a bat in the night the soul flies to God. Through the dark tunnel wherein was slime and filth, the soul emerges, clean, renewed, as a rainbow in the sky. As a rock is washed by the sea, so is the soul loved by God. The waves caress, they beat, they sleep. They come over and over again, the tide is full, the soul is engulfed. The tide is out, the soul waits.

As a lover to his bride, Christ holds the soul unto His lips. There is no wall, no fence, love flows free, as a colt from out the stable. The wind blows, across the plains of the world: anger is resolved. Man may eat.

The wind sweeps the wheat, warm, ripe: bread for the body, life for the soul.

1970

THE SPIRIT – II*

As we become more aware of our own depths do
we more consciously know where we are going, and
what we are doing?

Jesus said,

'I will hit with many stripes those that do evil
knowing they do evil.

Those who do evil not knowing they do evil I will
hit with a few stripes.'

We are meant to know, to learn, what we are doing.
My whole time I feel, of 'going Down', of intense
withdrawal, has been a means to this end.

The regression – Jesus said,

'Unless you become as little children' — was a part
of it.

There are no boundaries, no frontiers, no
walls to God – to the Spirit – to the Love of Christ.

As we become more free, more consciously aware,
so do we find, and use, external circumstances for
our own good, that is, as part of our movement toward
God.

The devil can only cause evil if you want evil. In
fragile, exposed, psychotic states the powers of
darkness are very real and menacing, within oneself

---

* In 1975 in London there was a Congress entitled
'Exploring the Ways of the Spirit'. Different people of different religions contributed. I was invited to speak in the
French Catholic Church called 'Notre Dame de France'
in Leicester Square. This writing was inspired by that event.

and around, outside. Nothing is covered, it is stark and raw.

The protection of our Lady I sought, the care of my Angel, I clung to, and of Saint Michael I could never ask enough.

The armour of God is not a hard shell; It is a shield of Love.

To cleave to God, to goodness, becomes a necessity, like bread and water.

Anger is a poison. We express it, we resolve it, we try not to 'get it'. As tiny babies, if much frustrated we got angry so often, so angry that it piled up inside, we couldn't express it all and sometimes such were our guilt feelings about expressing it, that we almost became mute statues.

Some may have called this 'good' and our crying and screaming 'bad'. In fact, it was better to be so called 'bad' and 'alive,' than 'good' and 'dead'.

We may have got into a habit of forgetting we wanted to scream but something in us remembered and the anger got stuck, in our guts – colitis – in our lungs – asthma, in our stomachs – ulcers, and so on.

Especially very early in life, can the anger poison come all 'in on you'. Until it is released or resolved you cannot Love freely and fully.

In a certain sense, all illness is psycho-somatic – it cannot be otherwise since we live Body *with* Soul – linked through the emotions.

Your Heart is always with you – so are your Brains, and one can get 'sore' and the other 'cramped' if you are unloved and told you are stupid.

A Schizophrenic can become a working machine, instead of a living human Being.

He is divided and if he refuses to go *through* this division he will stagnate, as a fish on dry land. The

split is his means of salvation, of reaching through
to God.

You swim underwater, you grope in the dark, you
seem to lose your way, your self and everything and
everyone. What you find is God. The Spirit was
always there in all the padding, and when that got
'blown off a bit' and you didn't grab it back on –
got smothered with distractions and noise, then if you
didn't get sick if you rested without physical illness,
and the break from 'normality' called 'madness' took
you as the current in a river, to the sea of your soul,
then you grew – you reached God.

In the end as in the beginning there is no need of
down or up: of germination and of bearing fruit. The
seed is always there and so is the fruit. The movement
and the stillness are together.

You lie in the agony of waiting and in the
contentment of completion.

You are together, whole. You are scattered, yet
complete.

You must be 'free' as the wind, yet completely tied
– to God – stuck as a limpet to Rock. You must strive
to see clearly, yet be blind and lead.

Such is the nature of the Path, such is the
way God made us.

The Spirit moves, the world flows, in and out, your
energy is spent yet remains, and is contained, as the
power in a seed.

NOTRE DAME DE FRANCE
FEAST OF THE SACRED HEART
6 JUNE, 1975

THE COMING OF
THE SPIRIT
Pentecost

As flames of fire into the heart, melting the hard wax,
the Spirit sears the soul, and it slips into the pool of
God. Where it is washed and cooled, as the meadow
sweet after rain, having a fragrance as of incense,
rising from the altar of the earth. As a beam of light
shot into the dark, from the door of God, the Spirit
comes. As light filtering through leaves does God
come into 'being'. As a cloud in the sky, God
overhangs the soul. As water is peat, God saturates
and seeps. As the surf of the sea does the Spirit come,
jubilant from the waves of God, to the sand of the
soul. The sand that shifts; that is washed, that is dry;
that is wet, that receives the sea; and is covered by
the sea.

BEING AND BECOMING

In all that is, He is, in all the space, beyond and
before. The world burns in His power and is
consumed in His Love.

I am leaving the lights of a town, they are fading,
before the moon and the stars, and in the dark, wrapt
in Christ; I feel the love of being.

I am high on a ship, leaving the people, tiny below,
moving away from the pull of the shore, I feel I am
floating, out to the open, to the sea, where I shall
be.

God, Love is within me and nought can take me
from that which dwells within.

In the wounds of the Passion am I buried, lost, as
nothing, and on the Cross do I live. He lifts me as
a babe, and in His strength do I dwell. He is my life,
as the earth is to the worm, as the sky is to a bird.

Everything that is: by its being, is bound to God.

By division, the splitting of the cell, and by
multiplication have I come from the piercing of the
seed.

So am I; pierced and split into the Body of Christ;
sleeping in His flesh, carried by His blood and
warmed by the glow of His sacred Heart.

Saint Lazarus pray for me that through Crucifixion
and Resurrection I may ascend ever nearer the shore,

the safe harbour of God, the Anchor of salvation.

God the beginning and the end of all. Of all seeking, of all knowing, of all Being.

CUD OF MY SOUL
(On the Food of a House)

O God, from the evil that I feel bring me to the heaven
I desire. Take thou my fear and in Thy hands spread
it before my eyes, that seeing with you that which
was hid I may be freed, that the flow of my love,
as a fountain released, may ascend in glory to the sky,
and fall, as Thy arms, to comfort crying souls. May
the agony of the Cross be the Gift of my life. It being
the path to the Resurrection. Through all the way,
meanderings, of this route, hold me to Thyself, the
kernel of my being. May the strength of goodness pull
me off the rocks, and the inner light of Thy knowledge
guide me, through the darkness of 'not knowing what
is happening'.

When I am lost in a multitude of screaming souls
– caught in silent bursting agonies, take thou my soul
and from it spread Thy peace.

From my heart clasp Thy love and with it ease the
torment, still the strife. Grant us Thy eyes to see what
is happening, and when in blind trust we stumble
about in the stubble of 'cut off lives' take Thou our
whole 'doings' and make of it a growth you alone
know how to make.

> Kneeling I worship,
> Bowed I love,
> Prostrate I adore.

O God, let me not flood – in a stew, all little bits

and pieces – but if I do, whisper in the chaos, 'no piece is lost, all that you have is mine and I always know where I put all my parts. Nothing is lost. All is part of a whole and the wholeness is me, Almighty God, who made thee.'

In the music of all your lives, concentrated as frozen ice, is the rhythm of my love. Its beat, its pulse, is warm to melt, to break through bars of iron, and walls of steel.

Creep near, before the Fire of my love and violent as the Flame of Truth shall I clutch the glowing embers of your souls, and from you shall burn a fire so brilliant, so piercing, that all my know that I, the Lord your God, brought you here; to your own lives.

DEATH

The floodgates of my soul are
open, and the water of my life, flows
out, into the endless sea of light.

LIGHT

The night is dark,
Yet shines, a gleaming
                    star,

And in the lapping of
                the waves,

Shall we hear the
            voice of GOD.

UNTITLED

Softly we touch,
   here, and there,
as the current
of our life, flows
   on its way

How lightly we step on the
                  sand.
– How soon comes the
            Tide.

BIBLIOGRAPHY

All books are published in London unless otherwise indicated.

American Psychiatric Association (1969) *A Psychiatric Glossary* (3rd edn). Washington, DC: American Psychiatric Association.

American Psychiatric Association (1980) *DSM-III: Diagnostic and Statistical Manual of Mental Disorders* (3rd edn). Washington, DC: American Psychiatric Association.

Barnes, Mary and Berke, Joseph (1971) *Mary Barnes: Two Accounts of a Journey Through Madness.* Harmondsworth: Penguin, 1973.

Berke, Joseph (1972) ' "Anti-psychiatry": an interview with Joseph Berke', in Boyers and Orrill, eds, pp. 209–17.

Boyers, Robert and Orrill, Robert, eds (1972) *Laing and Anti-psychiatry.* Harmondsworth: Penguin.

Clare, Anthony (1985) *In the Psychiatrist's Chair* (interview with R. D. Laing). BBC Radio, 14 July 1985.

Coles, Robert, Farber, Leslie H., Friedenberg, Edgar Z. and Lux, Kenneth (1972) 'R. D. Laing and anti-psychiatry: a symposium', in Boyers and Orrill, eds, pp. 157–80.

Cooper, J. E. (1989) 'An overview of the prospective ICD-10 classification of mental disorders', *British Journal of Psychiatry* 154: 21–3.

Cooper, Robin (1989) 'Beginnings', in Cooper and others, pp. 15–30.

Cooper, Robin and others (1989) *Thresholds between Philosophy and Psychoanalysis: Papers from the Philadelphia Association.* Free Association Books.

Dalley, Tessa, ed. (1984) *Art as Therapy: An Introduction to the Use of Art as a Therapeutic Technique.* Tavistock.

Duncan, J. Ann (1989) Review of Lindsay Knight, *Talking to a Stranger: A Consumer's Guide to Therapy*, *Free Associations* 15: 134–43.

Edgar, David (1979) *Mary Barnes* (playscript).

Farber, Leslie (1972) 'Schizophrenia and the mad psychotherapist', in Boyers and Orrill, eds, pp. 77–98.

Finlay, Marike (1989) 'Post-modernizing psychoanalysis/psychoanalysing post-modernity', *Free Associations* 16: 43–80.

Goffman, Erving (1961) *Asylums: Essays on the Social Situation of Mental Patients and Other Inmates.* New York: Anchor/Doubleday.

Gorden, Jan B. (1972) 'The meta-journey of R. D. Laing, in Boyers and Orrill, eds, pp. 48–76.

Gralnick, Alexander, ed. (1969) *The Psychiatric Hospital as a Therapeutic Instrument: Collected Papers of High Point Hospital.* New York: Brunner/Mazel, especially Ch. 3, 'In-patient psychoanalytic psychotherapy of schizophrenia: problem areas and perspectives', pp. 30–44.

Guattari, Félix (1984) *Molecular Revolution: Psychiatry and Politics.* Harmondsworth: Penguin.

Guimón, José (1989) 'The biases of psychiatric diagnosis', *British Journal of Psychiatry* 154: 33–7.

Harvard Medical School (1989) 'Families in the treatment of schizophrenia – Part 2', *Harvard Medical School Mental Health Letter* (July) 6: 1–3.

Judd, Dorothy (1985) Review of Tessa Dalley, ed. *Art as Therapy: An Introduction to the Use of Art as a Therapeutic Technique*, *British Journal of Psychotherapy* 2: 145–51.

Laing, R. D. (1960) *The Divided Self.* Tavistock.

—— (1967) *The Politics of Experience and The Bird of Paradise.* Harmondsworth: Penguin.

Lemoine-Luccioni, Eugénie (1987) *The Dividing of Women or Woman's Lot*, trans. M.-L. Davenport and M.-C. Réguis. Free Association Books.

Lidz, Theodore (1972) 'Schizophrenia, R. D. Laing and the Contemporary treatment of psychosis: an interview with Dr Theodore Lidz', in Boyers and Orrill, eds, pp. 123–56.

Menzies, Isabel (1959) 'The functioning of social systems as a defence against anxiety', in *Containing Anxiety in Institutions*. Free Association Books, 1988, pp. 43–85.

Mitchell, Juliet (1974) *Psychoanalysis and Feminism*. New York: Vintage, 1975.

Muller, Theresa Grace (1962) *Fundamentals of Psychiatric Nursing: A Guide to Nursing in Mental Illness*. Paterson, NJ: Littlefield, Adams.

Oakley, Chris (1989) Review of Claire Baron, *Asylum to Anarchy*, *Free Associations* 15: 108–25.

Oakley, Haya (1989) 'Touching and being touched: the negotiated boundaries and the "extended" consulting room', in Cooper and others, pp. 146–66.

Robertson, James and Robertson, Joyce (1989) *Separation and the Very Young*. Free Association Books.

Robinson, Alice M. (1964) *The Psychiatric Aide: A Textbook of Patient Care* (3rd edn). Philadelphia: J. B. Lippincott.

Schatzman, Morton (1972) 'Madness and morals', in Boyers and Orrill, eds, pp. 181–208.

Schwartz, Morris S. and Stanton, Alfred H. (1950) 'A social psychological study of incontinence', *Psychiatry* 13: 399–416.

Sedgwick, Peter (1972) 'R. D. Laing: self, symptom and society', in Boyers and Orrill, eds, pp. 11–47.

Segal, Abraham (dir.) (1986) *Colours Folly* (video film). First festival selection Cinema du Réel, Centre Georges Pompidou, Paris, 1987.

Shader, R., ed. (1981) *Manual of Psychiatric Therapeutics*. Boston, MA: Little, Brown.

Shader, R. I. and Jackson, Anthony H. (1981) 'Approaches to schizophrenia', in Shader, ed., pp. 63–100.

Siegler, Miriam, Osmond, Humphry and Mann, Harriet (1972) 'Laing's models of madness', in Boyers and Orrill, eds, pp. 99–122.

Spitzer, Stephan P. and Denzin, Norman K., eds (1968) *The Mental Patient: Studies in the Sociology of Deviance*. New York: McGraw-Hill.

Stanton, Alfred H. and Schwartz, Morris S. (1954) *The Mental Hospital: A Study of the Institutional Participation in Psychiatric Illness and Treatment*. New York: Basic.

Sullivan, Harry Stack (1953) *Conceptions of Modern Psychiatry: The First William Alanson White Memorial Lectures* (4th edn). New York: Norton.

Symington, Neville (in press) Review of Michael P. Carroll, *The Cult of the Virgin Mary*, *Free Associations* 19.

Winnicott, D. W. (1974) 'Fear of breakdown', *International Review of Psycho-Analysis* 1: 103–7.

USEFUL ADDRESSES

The Arbours Association
41 Weston Park
London NW8

The Philadelphia Association
4 Marty's Yard
17 Hampstead High Street
London NW3 1PX

The Shealin Trust
14 Kelvin Drive
Kelvinside
Glasgow G20 8QU